Survival Secrets

Critical life saving skills from Canada's leading expert on extreme outdoor survival training

Brian Emdin

What you don't know can hurt you.
This book could save your life. Period.

Copyright 2002 by Spotted Cow Press.

Spotted Cow Press Ltd.
4216 - 121 Street
Edmonton, Alberta, Canada T6J 1Y8
www.spottedcowpress.ca

National Library of Canada Cataloguing in Publication Data

Emdin, Brian, 1944-
  Survival secrets / Brian Emdin ; edited by Marilyn Florence ; illustrated by Melanie Eastley and Caitlin Wells.

Second printing.

ISBN: 0-9694665-5-2

1. Wilderness survival. I. Florence, Marilyn. II. Title.
GV200.5.E42 2002   613.6'9   C2002-911346-6

All rights reserved. No part of this publication may be reproduced, stored in a retrieval system, or transmitted in any form by any means whatsoever without prior permission of the copyright owners.

Printed and bound in Canada.

Edited by	Marilyn Florence, Edmonton, Alberta
Designed by	Melanie Eastley, Edmonton, Alberta
Illustrated by	Melanie Eastley and Caitlin Wells, Edmonton, Alberta
Composition by	Lu Ziola, Edmonton, Alberta
Cover insert photo by	Jon Harbourne, Edmonton, Alberta

contents

Foreword v

A Note to Survival Instructors vii
    The importance of learning the drill! vii

1. What is Survival? 1
    Dealing with loss of control 2
    Post-accident phases 2

2. An Ounce of Prevention 5
    Threat recognition 5
    An example: Monitoring weather 6
    Survival clothing 8
    The ideal survival clothing 8
    A word about cotton 10
    Specialty clothing for extreme conditions 10
    Footwear and headgear 11
    Commercial travel 12
    Emergency equipment 12
    Appropriate equipment 13
    Recommended survival equipment 14
    A word about survival kits 17
    Lost or broken eye glasses 17

3. The Survival Plan 19

4. First Aid ... .23
Types of first aid ... .23
Take advantage of adrenaline ... .25
Handling a common trio of problems ... .27
The benefits of following the survival plan ... .28

5. Fire ... .29
Why is fire so important in the survival plan? ... .29
If you cannot build a fire… ... .30
The psychological benefits of a survival fire ... .31
Fire starting ... .32
Survival fire requirements ... .32
Feather sticks ... .32
A tribute to feather sticks ... .35
Gathering firewood ... .36
Selecting a fire site ... .38
Convection, conduction and radiant heat ... .39
Reflecting wall: making the most of radiant heat ... .41
Lighting a fire ... .42

6. Shelter ... .47
The lean-to ... .48
Shelter site selection ... .49
The single person lean-to ... .51
The bough bed ... .52
Snow shelters ... .53
Shelters and long-term survival ... .56

7. Signals ... .59
Effective survival signals speed rescue ... .59
Survival signals ... .59
Saved by a failing signal ... .60
What do rescuers see? ... .61

8. Water **65**
    The importance of water in survival 65
    How long can you live without water? 65
    Thirst and dehydration 66
    How you lose water in survival 67
    Water quality and safety 68
    A delicate subject 69
    Simple water gathering techniques 70
    Reducing water loss 72
    Motion sickness and dehydration 73
    Dehydration can kill quickly 74
    Minimising dehydration 76

9. Food **77**
    Hunger and survival 77
    How long can you live without food? 77
    To eat or not to eat... 78

10. Foraging **81**
    Foraging benefits and dangers 81
    Foraging checklist 82
    Respect the law of diminishing returns 83
    Simple weapons and snares 83
    Snaring tactics 87
    Preparing your catch 87
    A word about hunting... 89

11. Survival Travel **91**
    Why travel in survival? 91
    The best survival travel check list 92
    Direction finding 93

12. Survival Psychology	.95
The crash	.95
Dealing with loss of control	.96
The will-to-live	.97
Unravelling the "will to live" mystery	.97
My will-to-live theory	.99
Psychological problems and solutions	.101
"The hump"	.103
Group psychology	.104
Dealing with difficult people	.105
13. Large Predators	.107
Bears	.107
Using pepper spray	.111
14. Surviving Insects	.113
Bug secrets	.114
Avoiding insects	.115
Clothing	.116
Insect repellents	.116
15. After the Rescue	.119
Post rescue collapse	.119
Remember!	.119
Post traumatic stress disorder	.119
16. Test your Survival Knowledge	.121
Case #1: The novice boaters	.121
Case #2: The professionals	.123
Afterword	.127

Foreword

Wilderness adventure is increasingly popular. Many of today's outdoor adventure seekers do not possess adequate knowledge, skills or the experience to avoid threat or manage an emergency. Without proper training there is a good chance that you will fail in a crisis. This book offers improved and simplified outdoor safety and survival training in the following areas:
- Threat recognition and avoidance
- Survival understanding and preparation
- Programming for effective response to an emergency
- Survival secrets

My wilderness and survival training experience spans fifty years, much of it in remote areas of northern Canada. During my tenure in the Canadian Forces Survival Training School, I discovered that survival training sometimes fails to adequately prepare people, and they subsequently perish in survivable circumstances.

Some survival training could better be described as "a camping trip where everyone forgets to bring food or a tent, but everyone brings along a fifty pound first aid kit." Outdoor emergencies require significantly more than just camping skills and first aid. Today's population is much more urban based than it was fifty years ago when the current survival-training model was developed. Many people facing a survival emergency today are unprepared for the psychological and physiological challenges. Some common survival problems, and their solutions, are presented here for the first time.

The following story is analogous to my survival training philosophy:

On a salmon river in Labrador, a guide navigated his boat through a treacherous stretch of rapids. His impressed client said, "You must know the location of every rock in those rapids." The guide replied, "No sir, I just know where a few of them aren't." You do not have to know everything about the wilderness in order to survive. You just have to know enough to avoid the rocks.

You are about to learn how to survive with virtually no specialised skills, experience, or equipment. The recommendations made here are simple, safe, easily performed, and effective. It is the best advice for everyone from novice to expert. This book is strongly recommended to anyone accepting an outdoors leadership role. On more than one occasion, survivors have claimed that my unique approach to survival training has saved their lives. Let's now prepare you for survival.

A Note to Survival Instructors

Survival and outdoor educators tend to be self reliant, confident, and skilled. It is difficult for some of these instructors to appreciate the diminished mental state and physical handicap that the average survivor must contend with. They are sometimes overly ambitious with their agenda. They often teach more than the student can absorb. Conventional survival training objectives are often unrealistic for injured or traumatised survivors. Basic survival instruction should teach skills that are simple, safe, effective, and easily performed.

Survival training should boost self-confidence. The instructor should not demonstrate unachievable skills. Survival students too often comment that they would be confident in survival provided they could bring along their instructors.

Teaching survival is a huge responsibility. Developing and maintaining an effective survival-training program requires constant research and an open mind. Sometimes instructors tenaciously adhere to tradition and stubbornly resist change despite evidence of superior methods.

Effective survival instruction requires repeating important teaching points. Instructors must ensure that the survival plan is memorised and internalised in the form of a drill.

The importance of learning the drill!

The following account illustrates the dramatic difference between effectively preparing for survival and failing to prepare. Two crewmembers were forced to eject from a jet fighter over the northern Canadian woods. It was in the dead of winter with temperatures approaching minus forty degrees.

One of the flyers fractured an ankle on landing. He immediately started a fire. He splinted his ankle in front of the fire and then continued the survival plan. He gathered enough firewood to last well through the night and then built a lean-to shelter. He kept the fire burning warm and brightly all night. He even built a pair of makeshift snowshoes.

He had watched his crewmate descend only a half-mile away. His concern grew because he had not seen any evidence of life coming from his friend's location. There was no light from a fire. There had been no flares, no shouts, or whistles in response to his many failed attempts to hail him. He concluded that his buddy must be injured and was determined to look for him the next day.

A high-flying search aircraft conducted a night visual and radio search along the downed aircraft's planned flight route. When morning dawned, a search and rescue helicopter arrived overhead. Their prompt arrival was a direct result of the fire being spotted during the night.

The injured flyer directed the helicopter to where he had seen his companion go down. The parachute was spotted quickly. The pilot was found frozen, sitting on the trunk of a fallen tree just a few steps from where he had landed. The autopsy revealed no injuries. The cause of death was never explained.

The tracks in the snow indicated that the pilot had walked directly to the fallen tree. He was undoubtedly experiencing some degree of post-mishap trauma. He certainly would have been chilled by the frigid descent. The cockpit emergency and subsequent ejection had guaranteed an abundance of adrenaline which he evidently failed to utilise.

I suspect the following sequence occurred. The trauma and lack of an action plan caused him to sit down on the fallen tree in a daze. He did not burn off his adrenaline and therefore suffered an attack of hypoglycaemia. The low blood sugar extended his lethargy. He advanced into and eventually succumbed to hypothermia.

An uninjured survivor died sitting on that log. If he had memorised the survival plan and understood the requirement to initiate it immediately I am convinced he would not have perished.

Why teach the survival plan as a drill?
- Memorising a simple plan will ensure rapid progress in a survival situation.
- Rapid progress will help regain a sense of control.
- Regaining a sense of control will boost confidence.
- Boosted confidence enables you think clearly, focus and concentrate.
- Clear thinking, focus and concentration enable you to innovate and effectively solve your unique survival problems.

What is Survival?

Survival is a complex concept that is not fully understood by most people. Clearly, you cannot adequately prepare for something you do not understand! Understanding survival is the first step in learning how to survive.

The following elements are common to most survival situations:
- you are in an immediate, life threatening, environmental situation
- you are traumatised to some degree both physiologically and psychologically. Varying degrees of trauma can result from events involving serious injury to nothing more than loss of controls and expectations such as locomotion, heat, light, and communication
- you do not know when or how your emergency situation will end
- you have lost control over many things that you normally take for granted, such as heat, light, comfort, agenda, communication, and transportation. Not knowing how or when your survival ordeal will end makes the loss of these controls more devastating
- you are confronted with harsh realities. (for example, death, injury, suffering and personal loss)
- you are in some level of denial. (Our common inability to accept mortality tends to create an attitude of denial. Denial frequently prevents timely recognition of required action in an emergency. Quick reaction is often vital to survival.)
- you are in an environmental emergency situation that could present problems requiring difficult personal decisions and tough humanitarian compromise
- you experience fear, anguish, and, possibly, remorse
- you must act promptly to avoid further threat or to extend life.

Considering all of these commonalities, I offer the following definition of survival:
Survival means doing everything possible to extend life just one moment longer.

Unfortunately, human problem-solving ability tends to be inversely proportional to the magnitude of the emergency. Trauma adversely affects your ability to set priorities and solve problems; thus, you are not likely to make logical and deliberate decisions in a crisis. Good emergency decisions are usually the result of advance preparation.

It is vital that you promptly accept and deal with your survival circumstances. There are numerous accounts of people giving up just minutes before rescue arrives. No matter how bleak your situation, you must never give up.

In this book you will learn how to overcome the psychological and physiological hurdles of a wilderness mishap or emergency. You also will learn how to program yourself so that you will act effectively and reliably in any survival emergency. Your survival preparation might benefit many other people besides yourself.

Dealing with loss of control

Loss of control in survival emergencies is frustrating, bewildering, and traumatising. Most of us require training to prepare for the harsh realities of a survival situation. Many victims die because of their failure to deal with lost control. *Stuff happens – get over it:* this is commonly given advice that doesn't help one bit. Two other pieces of frequent and ineffective advice are "Don't panic" and "Remain calm."

Only the implementation of an effective survival plan will enable you to quickly regain lost control in an emergency. Coincidentally, it will also control panic and help you remain calm. This subject will be covered again in Chapter 12 (Survival Psychology).

Post-accident phases

After any serious mishap survivors generally go through the following phases. They spend varying amounts of time in each, but they experience them all.

The unprepared accident survivor invariably loses precious time and opportunity by struggling through all of the following post-accident phases. The advice in this book is designed to program you to accept a survival situation immediately and take full advantage of fleeting opportunities.

> **Shock.** "What happened?" Initially people are unable to understand what has occurred. Accident victims often fail to realise immediately the extent of their injuries or the magnitude of the situation.
> **Denial.** "This can't be happening!" This stage is one of stunned disbelief. The enormity or reality of the situation overwhelms the victims and they often refuse to accept their situation or loss.
> **Anger.** "This shouldn't be happening!!" This stage results in frustration, rage, or blame directed at fate or circumstances.
> **Acceptance.** In this last stage, casualties, injuries, and further danger are finally accepted. Only in this final stage does the survivor do anything to improve his or her situation. Unfortunately, many survival opportunities are lost because they are available only in the first few minutes after an accident!

The following list of survival training requirements represents the ingredients crucial to your survival. You will:
1. learn to recognise and to avoid potential survival situations or threats
2. develop the minimum skills, knowledge, and experience to deal with an unavoidable survival emergency
3. learn to program yourself to recognise a survival emergency and immediately initiate and complete the memorised survival plan.

I have dealt with these requirements in the following chapters. Chapter 2 deals with preparedness, focusing on threat recognition, and clothing and equipment selection. Chapter 3 introduces you to the survival plan, and Chapters 4 through 9 address components of the plan. Chapters 10 through 14 feature information on foraging, survival travel, survival psychology, large predators, and insects. Chapter 15 addresses post-rescue issues. Finally, Chapter 16 gives you a chance to test your survival knowledge.

Studies indicate that humans are inexplicably lucky in their encounters with danger. Nearly all of us make it through life with our eyesight, and our fingers and toes intact, despite the countless occasions when we jeopardise our safety. Most fatalities are the result of a series of avoidable mistakes and overlooked warnings. If you learn to recognise and avoid threatening situations, and if you are properly equipped and prepared, most outdoor misadventures will result in nothing more serious than an unscheduled camping experience.

Survival review
- understand that survival relates to an imminent threat
- survival depends upon the timely recognition of a threat plus immediate action
- survival usually requires overcoming an extreme mental and physical ordeal
- survival requires the reconciliation of personal loss
- survival requires the determination to regain control by maximising minimal resources
- survival is not a matter of common sense! Survival depends upon knowledge, skills, and experience
- a committed and memorised plan is the best preparation for a survival emergency

An Ounce of Prevention

Threat recognition

Humans tend to disregard threat and rationalise inaction. As a group, we deny the immediacy and danger of the situation – for instance, most of us ignore fire alarms in public buildings and fail to exit immediately. Indeed, the potential threat of total destruction of home, neighbourhood or community is often too difficult to grasp. We have only to look to history, however, to see the effect of disregarding warnings about impending natural disasters. Entire communities have perished because a threat was unheeded.

An effective warning that results in action requires the following components:
1. a loud warning (bell, siren, and the like)
2. a visual warning (for example, flashing lights)
3. an audible description of the danger
4. clear and stern directions
5. warning of the consequences of failing to comply.

Unfortunately, you are not likely to receive the above warning in most situations. You must program yourself to detect danger and react to less effective warnings. You must monitor the following factors on a regular basis:
- weather
- environment, including such factors as avalanche risk
- progress
- resources
- fitness
- time and daylight remaining
- dehydration, fatigue, hypothermia

An example: monitoring weather

Hypothermia is caused by exposure to weather and is the biggest killer in survival. That is why weather leads the list of factors that you must monitor on a regular basis. The following are indicators that the weather is changing. Be prepared to take immediate action.

Weather changes
- wind direction change
- sky change (amount of cloud cover, type of cloud, dark cloud)
- temperature drop
- precipitation
- pressure change

A rapid drop in barometric pressure usually foreshadows bad weather. Pressure changes can be detected. As the atmospheric pressure drops, gases are released from the earth and water. You can smell these gases. Have you ever noticed an earthy smell in the air just prior to a thunderstorm? That awareness could enable you to seek shelter and avoid a survival situation. The point is that there will always be valuable information available. Learn as much as you can and pay attention to all of your senses.

The benefits of developing observation skills extend beyond safety. They are the secret to success for many outdoor activities including fishing, hunting, trapping, or nature watching. Most survival situations are avoidable. Faithfully use the monitoring system above to detect potential threat.

"Hope for the best but prepare for the worst."

By simply dressing adequately, packing sufficient equipment and stowing it securely you will be acknowledging the potential of an outdoor emergency. Taking precautions will help program you to watch for signs of danger. Your vigilance must be followed by action: you must also program yourself to take immediate action when you recognise a threat. Whoever coined the saying "an ounce of prevention is worth a pound of cure" must have been thinking about survival.

In summary, you should use this checklist to program yourself for an emergency.
- establish personal emergency procedures
- memorise these procedures in a simple drill
- program yourself to recognise threat warning
- resolve to act when warned or threatened

Man, mouse – or moose?

Driving emergencies require the effective use of emergency programming. Your first priority in driving should be to concentrate on safeguarding human lives. You simply cannot depend upon instinctive reactions in an emergency. You can, however, train and program yourself to react quickly and appropriately when the situation warrants.

The following advice defines my personal driving philosophy: Swerve for a moose; do not swerve for a mouse. You do not want to hit a moose – or any object that weighs as much as your automobile. Vehicle collisions with moose are frequently fatal for the vehicle occupants. I advocate aggressive moose avoidance manoeuvres. They warrant the associated risk. On the other hand, you cannot justify risking human lives by swerving out of control to avoid hitting a small animal.

Internalise the moose or mouse scenario so that you can quickly assess your options in a driving emergency and take appropriate action. Without this programming, most driving emergencies rarely graduate beyond a gasp, a death grip on the steering wheel, and target fixation.

Survival clothing

A well-prepared outdoor enthusiast will be clothed and equipped to meet any reasonable contingency. Survival emergencies have an annoying habit of occurring when people have insufficient equipment and are wearing inadequate clothing. Many situations would not be classified as survival if the individuals were adequately clothed and equipped.

Consider the following points when choosing your outdoor clothing:
- type of adventure planned
- level of participation
- climate, season and potential weather extremes
- type of transportation
- type of terrain to be crossed and or encountered
- duration of activity
- separation from civilization.

Survival secret

Adequate clothing and equipment minimises your survival threat.

The ideal survival clothing

Exposure to cold, wind, rain or snow, water (immersion), heat and sun may have devastating consequences. You may experience accelerated loss of body heat. This results in the condition known as hypothermia, which is the biggest killer in survival situations. Exposure also accelerates loss of energy and moisture reserves, causing dehydration.

The ideal survival clothing will:
- block the wind
- insulate against cold
- minimise perspiration loss
- keep out rain and snow
- provide floatation
- be comfortable, strong, and flexible, but not too bulky
- allow excess body heat to vent or dissipate

Amazing advances are being made in high-tech fabrics and insulating materials. Clothing technology will soon enable us to safely participate in activities that would have previously threatened our survival. Nonetheless, until the perfect survival clothing is invented, we should apply the tried and true principle of layering clothing. Layering allows for flexibility both in changing conditions and in emergencies. It allows you to dry out some clothing while continuing to wear protection from the elements.

The following lists identify the ideal qualities for each layer of clothing.

The outer layer
- single layer shell
- strong
- windproof
- waterproof
- loose fitting
- easily ventilated
- easily stowed

The middle layer(s)
- breathable
- insulating, even when wet
- easily ventilated
- quick drying
- hydrophobic (repels water to outside)
- strong
- loose fitting (create dead air space)
- light
- washable

The inner layer
- wicks moisture away from your body
- insulates when wet
- dries quickly
- feels soft, comfortable, non-chafing
- does not restrict movement

A word about cotton

Cotton clothing is not recommended for wilderness wear. This includes cotton undergarments. Cotton absorbs and holds moisture. It dries slowly and is non-insulating and uncomfortable when wet. We all love cotton denim jeans, but I cannot stress too vehemently: *do not wear denim jeans in the wilderness.* (If you insist upon going to the field in jeans you might as well pin a note on your back that says: "My jeans have caused self-inflicted hypothermia. Do not render assistance.")

Many modern synthetics provide better alternatives. Some occupations require static free or fire retardant inner or outer clothing for which synthetics pose a dilemma. Regulations or your personal threat assessment will dictate any required compromise.

Specialty clothing for extreme conditions

Some very low-tech foam materials are sometimes used in arctic garments. This type of clothing will keep you warm in extreme cold, even if you get wet, but it tends to be bulky in active situations. Excellent sea survival suits are available for boaters. (Immersion in cold water without thermal protection results in rapid onset of hypothermia.) Proper clothing can extend your survivability to a matter of days, verses minutes or hours.

There are many types of breathable waterproof materials on the market that claim to keep out water while allowing water vapour (perspiration) to escape. Some materials I have experimented with are indeed waterproof. Unfortunately they do not allow moisture to escape very effectively. They do not work well in cold or even cool weather. Perspiration vapour tends to condense on the inner side of the cold outer surface.

Waterproofing is not generally required in the winter arctic. Moisture in the outer layers turns to ice crystals, which eventually will sublimate (change from ice to water vapour) in a cold dry climate. You can hang clothing in the dry arctic wind to accelerate sublimation and also partially remove ice by knocking the ice crystals out of footwear and clothing.

Footwear and headgear

You can avoid a tremendous amount of heat loss by protecting your head and neck from exposure. You should protect your head, feet and hands at least as well, if not better, than you protect the rest of your body.

Footwear should fit properly and afford protection relative to your activity and the terrain you will be travelling. The presence of rocks, cold, water, snakes, insects, and slippery conditions will influence your choice of footwear.

Socks should be given as much consideration as outer footwear. They should wick away moisture, thus preventing heat loss, blisters, and moisture damage to your skin. Socks should be durable, insulating when wet, and quick drying. If possible, bring an extra pair of socks.

> **Survival secret**
>
> Protect your feet.

Layer cold weather headgear. The inner layer should be made of wicking material that retains insulating properties when wet, and dries quickly. It should have adequate and well-positioned eyeholes and you should be able to pull the inner layer completely over your face. The outer layers should be insulated and wind proof. The hood of your parka should extend well beyond your face to create a snorkel opening. This provides a dead air space that is warmed by your breath and prevents frostbite, dehydration, and body heat loss. The snorkel hood can be made adjustable by inserting a length of suitable wire inside the outer edge. You can then change the shape of the hood to dramatically improve protection from a side wind; for instance, you can extend the windward side and close the opposite side in towards your face and thus avoid frostbite.

Animal fur is commonly used to trim parka hoods. The long guard hairs of some animals (such as wolverine) do not tend to frost up from your breath. When the hood is closed the hairs mesh. This creates a warm buffer. It also diffuses bright sunlight and offers some protection from snow blindness.

Your psychological and physiological well-being can be affected dramatically by your clothing. This is true whether you are struggling to enjoy an outdoor activity during inclement weather or attempting to survive in an emergency. Properly prepared outdoors enthusiasts will select clothing that protects them in the worst-case scenario. Remember: always wear clothing that accommodates a change in the weather or a mishap.

Commercial travel

Commercial travel requires innovative survival planning. Consider possible emergencies when you dress to travel. Be reasonable. It is impossible to dress for every conceivable survival extreme that might be encountered on a winter flight from Northern Canada to Hawaii. I always wear winter boots when I travel in cold weather and keep my parka with me at my seat.

Emergency equipment

Frequently, the mishap that creates the survival situation also separates you from stowed emergency equipment. Be a minimalist: *depend only upon the survival equipment on your person*. When I fly commercial airlines, I wear a multi-pocketed suede vest that discreetly holds my survival items. I carry as much equipment as practical. I choose multi-purpose items that are small and light, and I make sure I can access and operate my vital survival equipment with either hand.

The *very least* you should carry when travelling is a knife and fire starting equipment. Current commercial transportation regulations do not permit you to carry a pocket-knife or other sharp instruments on your person. Carry a pocket-knife in your checked luggage. It will serve your needs in a survival emergency. You should also carry waterproof, windproof matches, or a cigarette lighter. Some people have waterproof matches sewn into the lining of their favourite outdoor clothing for emergencies. This reduces the temptation to use the matches in non-emergency situations.

You have a tremendous psychological advantage if you are determined to survive with only a knife and matches. With this mindset, any additional equipment you have in survival would be considered a bonus and would boost your morale. Maximise your ingenuity. Foam is commonly used in the seat cushions of virtually every form of transportation. It is nearly always overlooked as a source of first aid material, footwear, clothing, bedding, or shelter.

Appropriate equipment

Some equipment is simply inappropriate in the hands of an inexperienced survivor. Chainsaws are a good example. There is another much simpler implement commonly used in conventional survival training that is very dangerous. The axe is an inappropriate tool in the hands of an inexperienced survivor, and it almost always produces negative results.

The axe has always been used in survival training. This is because survival training was developed for the benefit of downed aircrew at a time when nearly everyone knew how to use an axe. When air regulators originally stipulated that all aircraft must carry an axe, it was a logical choice.

Today's urban survival students look forward to the prospect of training with an axe. The axe is a time machine. With your first swing you are transported back in time. You are instantly standing shoulder to shoulder with prominent frontier heroes who have been immortalised in outdoor history and folklore. Unfortunately, today's survival students have little or no experience in safe axe handling. I have witnessed many accidents and near misses related to axe use. Inexperienced axe users tend to:
- work too hard or too fast for safety
- develop blisters
- become quickly fatigued without stopping to rest and recover
- overexert themselves until they are perspiring profusely
- injure themselves or others

Improper axe handling will seriously deplete your quick energy reserves (glycogen) within just a few minutes. This will cause the rapid onset of fatigue. Excessive sweating leads to dehydration. Sweating also makes your clothes and hair damp; this increases heat loss and hastens hypothermia. Hypothermia, dehydration, and fatigue all adversely affect your ability to focus and concentrate.

Safe axe handling requires considerable focus and concentration, which are not attributes associated with a survival victims' trauma.

While there is absolutely nothing wrong with learning how to use an axe, it takes time and much practice. Unless you have used an axe all your life, it is best not use an axe in survival if it can be avoided. Most survival tasks can be accomplished more safely and more efficiently without an axe. A knife will function adequately in survival.

Survival secret

It is psychologically devastating to injure yourself unnecessarily in survival.

Recommended survival equipment

The following survival items could be considered for carrying on your person during outdoor activities, including camping, fishing, hiking, boating, hunting, cross-country skiing, climbing, etc. There will undoubtedly be other items that you require personally that you can add to this list. Make sure you select sturdy, reliable equipment.

Useful survival items
- **waterproof, windproof matches.** Make sure you can access and open them with either hand. Use plastic photography film canisters since they float, are waterproof and can be opened with one hand. Use only for emergencies.
- sturdy, multifunction **pocket-knife** that can be accessed and opened with either hand
- large, sturdy, bright **orange plastic bag.** Useful for rain, snow, and wind protection, signaling, carrying water, as a sail, etc.

- **sturdy multifunction tool** that can be accessed and opened with one hand
- **mechanical pencil** with extra stored lead (I wrap various size sewing needles to the pencil with heavy nylon thread, stainless steel wire, Teflon and duct tape.) Teflon tape will often repair leaking threaded joints or stripped threads. This could help you repair your motorised equipment and get you out of your survival situation
- **small note pad** in a re-sealable, heavy, waterproof, plastic bag
- **flashlight** (small, waterproof, brightly coloured, extra bulb and long-life batteries taped to flashlight with lots of tape that is useful in emergencies). A small light can be held in your mouth, leaving both hands free. They are available with adjustable beam width. If the flashlight is not brightly coloured, wrap some fluorescent tape around it
- **bandages** (stretch, bandanna, duct tape, mole skin, butterfly, etc.)
- **medicinal items:** medicine, lip balm, sun screen, insect repellent, small vile of ammonia for insect bites and stings, small tube of antiseptic and antibiotic cream, Vaseline-impregnated gauze packet (for medical use, fire starting, candle or equipment lubrication), inhalers, nasal spray, pain killers, chronic disease medication. (Select very small containers of medicinal items so that they will fit comfortably in your pockets and not weigh you down. Check all medication prior to each outing to ensure that it is not time expired, damaged, or depleted.)
- **reflective Mylar plastic bag** for signaling, water collection, and covering sucking chest wounds (an empty large potato chip bag)
- **compass and topographical map**
- **watch**
- **tube of quick-drying, strong, flexible cement** to repair or seal equipment, footwear or clothing
- **spare eyeglasses**
- **plastic magnifier** (light weight)
- **radio, cellular phone, GPS** (global position system) spare long-life batteries

Survival Secrets

- parachute **cord**, strong Nylon, Dacron or other more modern ultra strength **fishing line**
- **needle and strong thread**
- **aluminum foil**
- **space blanket** (small package of thin reflective plastic)
- **candles**
- plastic-handled, folding lock-blade **camp saw** (not allowed on airlines)
- **snare wire** (picture-hanging wire)

Know how to use your survival equipment and know where it is stowed. Some people wear a multi-pocket vest or fanny pack (over or under clothing) to hold their survival items. The benefit to this system is that your survival items are always available. Others choose loose fitting clothing with large secure pockets. Loose fitting clothing insulates well and is comfortable. It also holds lots of emergency equipment without becoming overly tight or restrictive. It is important that you become familiar with each item and its location.

I duplicate critical items such as matches and knife, and carry them on opposite sides of my body. If I sustain damage or injury to one side, I have a back up resource that I can still reach.

In a survival emergency, take stock of every piece of equipment. Check every pocket. If possible, securely attach critical items (knife, compass, flashlight) with a line to your clothing. This will prevent losses and delays while you prepare camp. Never use your knife while it is attached to you by a cord. You will inevitably reach out to cut something and slice your hand open. You can form a loop in the knife cord so that you can quickly and easily free it from your person.

Survival secret: inventory your possessions

Take the time to inventory every single item in your possession down to the gum wrapper you conscientiously pocketed to avoid littering. These items constitute all your worldly possessions. Discard nothing. Everything you have may be useful and not necessarily as originally intended. If the woods are wet and you have a dry twenty dollar bill in your pocket then roll it up and use it to light your fire. It will be the best twenty dollar investment you ever make.

A word about survival kits

Survival kits tend to be assembled or purchased and then ignored. We tend to forget about or be unfamiliar with the equipment in the kit. Some of the items may become damaged or spoiled (time expired). People tend to put poor quality items in survival kits. It is hard to put a $75 knife in a kit you hope you never have to use.

Lost or broken eye glasses

In an emergency you can use a pinhole in paper or other thin material to adjust your focus to enable you to read medicine labels, repair, operating or emergency instructions. You can also use this technique to repair equipment. If you are unable to produce a pinhole apparatus, you can create a magnifying pinhole between your thumb and first two fingers.

Survival secret

Always carry critical survival gear on your person.

Survival review

You cannot predict the circumstances of your survival ordeal. Dress adequately. Make a habit of carrying all the items that you might need in an emergency. With adequate equipment, some potential survival situations will be reduced to an inconvenience instead of an emergency.

The Survival Plan

The survival plan described in this book is the most effective plan in any environmental emergency. It establishes priorities and can save your life in a survival situation.

This simple survival plan does not rely upon detailed techniques or specialised equipment. In an actual survival situation, rapid progress builds confidence. Confidence helps you to concentrate, to focus, and to think clearly. These attributes significantly increase your ability to innovate and effectively solve problems.

The survival plan
1. first aid
2. fire
3. shelter
4. signals
5. water
6. food

You must memorise the plan: this will program you to function effectively even if you are traumatised. You must commit yourself to initiate the plan immediately in a survival situation and to complete it without deviation. Keep the entire survival plan in perspective. Avoid spending too much time and energy on any one endeavour. You will read this advice several times throughout this book. Repetition will help program you for survival.

You must execute the plan in sequence. You may not be injured and therefore may be tempted to by-pass first aid; however, survival first aid includes checking for danger to yourself and others before continuing with the survival plan. You must ensure that people or resources remaining in a damaged aircraft or vehicle are safe from further danger. Proceed as quickly as possible with the survival plan but frequently recheck the plan from the beginning to ensure you have not missed a crucial element. For instance, initial first aid may require further treatment later.

The items in the survival plan are closely connected. Many times fire is your primary first aid requirement in a survival situation: most people die from hypothermia or loss of body core temperature in survival circumstances. Heroic medical measures often save lives in emergencies; however, these efforts would be wasted if the entire group subsequently perished from hypothermia. For this reason fire must always be considered before shelter and immediately after first aid. In desert survival, dehydration certainly contributes to death, but victims still expire at night from hypothermia. Even in the desert you will need to address body heat loss.

The sequence of priorities in the survival plan has stood the test of time. Do not consider reinventing the survival plan in an emergency. Throughout this book the survival plan will be used as a guide to address a variety of survival situations.

Survival secret

Memorise the survival plan. It doesn't weigh anything. It doesn't take any space. You can't lose it or forget to pack it. It will be your most valuable asset if you are ever faced with survival.

The following example is typical of what often happens in actual survival situations when the survival plan is not followed faithfully. A hunter had an accident while driving his all-terrain vehicle in a remote area. He was badly shaken up, but there was no immediate evidence of injury. The all-terrain vehicle was damaged beyond repair. It was late in the afternoon. The hunter recognised that at least one night in the woods was inevitable. It was a warm, sunny, September day. He unwisely started building a shelter rather than first starting a fire and then collecting an overnight supply of firewood. This was contrary to the survival plan.

The accident had produced a significant amount of adrenaline. About fifteen minutes after the accident, the pain killing effects of the adrenaline began to dissipate. He then felt a stabbing pain. Adrenaline had masked the pain from an undetected broken ankle. The pain quickly became intolerable. He could not proceed until the injured ankle was immobilised and properly supported with a walking splint.

This injury delay was just the beginning of the survivor's problems. The weather took a turn for the worse: the temperature dropped twenty degrees and a rainsquall arrived. The hunter had no choice but to suffer in the cold and wet while he administered a splint to his ankle. Meanwhile, the abundant dry tinder, kindling and firewood was being drenched.

By not following the survival plan this injured hunter was soon wet, miserable and facing a serious survival threat. He was forced to hobble around in pain looking for splint materials. He had to sit in the cold driving rain while he applied the splint. He was then forced to painfully and laboriously gather fuel in a downpour. Attempting to produce dry tinder and light a fire under those conditions is not an enviable task.

This hunter learned the hard way that an emergency is not a good time to reinvent the survival plan. He made the almost fatal mistake of following the survival plan out of sequence. In good weather survivors often lose their sense of urgency. They don't complete the plan quickly. But why tempt fate in a survival situation? If you were having a lucky day you wouldn't be in a survival situation in the first place. By all means "hope for the best, but plan for the worst."

Survival secret

Don't tempt fate when she has already indicated that she is in a bad mood.

Survival review
1. memorise the survival plan:
    - first aid
    - fire
    - shelter
    - signals
    - water
    - food
2. initiate the plan immediately
3. complete the plan
4. don't take shortcuts or deviate from the plan

First Aid

In this chapter you will learn the difference between survival first aid and other forms of first aid. Please note that the following advice is my personal opinion and I am not a medical or first aid professional. You should obtain current first aid training.

> **The survival plan**
> 1. first aid
> 2. fire
> 3. shelter
> 4. signals
> 5. water
> 6. food

Types of first aid

Most survival training teaches only standard and wilderness first aid. You also must be prepared to apply survival first aid.

Standard first aid is intended to provide stopgap medical treatment until professional medical expertise can be obtained.

Wilderness first aid advocates a more in-depth treatment because professional medical care may be delayed or is inaccessible. (Wilderness first-aid preparedness is essential for the outdoor enthusiast. Take advantage of this type of training if it is available in your area. You can also ask your local medical emergency professionals where you can obtain first aid instructional guides.)

Survival first aid requires the treatment and protection of injuries (i.e. stabilisation of the victim) in a manner that allows you to complete the survival plan. Survival first aid often requires compromise and difficult choices. You have to be prepared to save life over limb. For instance, you might have to apply a tourniquet to reduce blood flow in an unconscious survivor. This action is not normally advocated but might be necessary if you need to save additional lives. A tourniquet may save the victim's life but cause the loss of the leg.

Acknowledging the unique requirements of survival first aid in advance will help program you to save lives in an emergency. Lives have undoubtedly been lost in survival because only conventional first aid was administered.

Not knowing when rescue or medical attention will arrive is one of the biggest challenges a survivor faces. Survivors frequently spend too much time and energy on first aid, because they assume that rescue is imminent. Failure to quickly proceed with the survival plan can result in tragic consequences.

Survival secret

If you are still alive thirty minutes after the accident, there is a 95% probability that you can survive for at least three days without further medical attention, but only if you complete the survival plan.

Typical survival failures
- the individual or group was inadequately trained and therefore psychologically unprepared to deal with the mishap
- the survival plan was not known, or not memorised
- the survival plan was not initiated immediately, resulting in critical delays
- the survivors did not recognise that first aid includes taking required action to protect from further injury
- too much time, energy and resources were expended on futile or unnecessary medical concerns, as well as other non-critical issues (When administering survival first aid, the law of diminishing returns must be respected)

Survival first aid action plan

To avoid the typical survival failures, apply the following measures:
- quickly survey the entire situation so that you can make effective survival decisions
- accept that there will likely be delays in receiving professional medical help
- make tough decisions involving compromise and sacrifice
- quickly evaluate, stabilise and protect injuries in a manner that allows continued survival activity
- complete the first aid treatment quickly so that you can proceed with the rest of the survival plan

Take advantage of adrenaline

If you have an accident that results in a survival situation, your body will undoubtedly experience a surge of adrenaline. Adrenaline is a powerful hormone known as the fight or flight stimulus. It significantly blocks pain. It gives you strength, energy, and the ability to think quickly. Adrenaline also stimulates your memory and allows the total recall of memorised drills – such as the survival plan!

Survival secret

Adrenaline boosts your memory.

As mentioned, it is common for adrenaline to initially block pain from injuries sustained in an accident. (Remember the hunter in the previous chapter!) For this reason, first aid should include periodic reassessment, rather than being checked off and forgotten. (Also consider the potential numbing effects of adrenaline that may be concealing an injury before you decide to travel any distance immediately after an accident.) You must initiate the survival plan immediately, and work quickly in order to take full advantage of any pain killing and energy boosting effects of adrenaline. If you work fast, much of the survival plan can be completed with the help of adrenaline.

Adrenaline also can play a negative role in survival. If you do not burn off adrenaline through immediate physical activity, you may suffer a low blood sugar condition. By not utilising your adrenaline you risk experiencing the following symptoms:

- loss of initiative
- loss of motivation
- loss of energy
- loss of the ability to plan
- loss of the ability to solve problems
- loss of ability to remain focused
- lowered morale
- diminished will-to-live

Survival secret

Adrenaline – get busy and use it!

The following scenario highlights the value of memorising an emergency plan and making the most of adrenaline. A military pilot was forced to ditch his aircraft at sea. His emergency egress and ditching training had included much repetition. The adrenaline rush helped him recall the escape plan so vividly that he claimed he could actually hear his instructor's voice calling out each step of the drill. He escaped from his submerged aircraft and swam to safety through a slick of burning fuel. He followed the drill precisely as he had practised it. The slightest deviation from the drill would have proven fatal. It had been twenty years since he had taken that emergency training. Take a lesson from this pilot: Memorise the survival plan and use it.

Handling a common trio of problems

Pain can run the gamut from distracting to completely debilitating. You can overcome pain by applying first aid, keeping busy, and focusing on something other than the pain. It is possible for pain to affect a larger area than the injury. This may be psychological pain. You can learn to narrow pain down to the specific injury area and then tune that area out.

Cold very often is localised in the hands or feet or one spot on your body. Like pain, cold can psychologically affect much larger areas. You can isolate the cold area and then tune it out. This will allow you to remain focused and solve problems. Cover your head and neck region and produce heat through physical activity. This is the best way to warm up if you cannot make a shelter or do not have an adequate source of external heat. Unprotected exposure to extreme cold will cause frostbite and hypothermia.

As you become chilled, it becomes progressively more difficult to move or to motivate yourself. The ability to separate psychological cold from the physical effects of cold will help your survival. You must force yourself to concentrate on survival requirements and block out the cold as much as possible.

Frostbite progresses from mild to more severe stages. Mild frostbite usually appears first on your cheeks, nose, and ears. The affected area will look waxy, white, and feel solid when touched. The warmth from your hand will take out mild frostbite instantly. If possible use the buddy system to monitor for frostbite. To warm frostbitten hands or feet, place them inside clothing in a warm area such as under your arms or those of your companion. Frostbitten skin is fragile and easily injured by heat or rough handling. If your feet or the feet of other survivors are deeply frostbitten, do not thaw them if you can wait for professional medical attention. Do not thaw frozen hands or feet if they are likely to refreeze.

Survival Secrets

The benefits of following the survival plan

In the ideal situation, you will have utilised the increased strength and energy benefit from adrenaline to expedite the survival plan. You will likely have both a fire and a good supply of fuel when the effect wears off. The fire will comfort and protect you while you administer first aid to previously undetected injuries. You will be able to comfortably stabilise your injuries and alleviate the pain. A cozy fire will also allow you to calmly re-assess your situation. Newly discovered injuries may dictate an adjustment to your planned survival activity. A fire will boost both your morale and confidence, which promotes survival-oriented innovation.

Remember: In an emergency situation, you will be administering first aid under duress and often without consultation. Resolve to be decisive and confident in your choice of action, and do not second guess yourself after the emergency abates. You will be performing in extraordinary circumstances and survival is your ultimate goal – concern yourself with extending life one moment longer!

Survival review

Remember these survival first aid actions:
- assess the total threat
- take the action that will save the most lives
- save life before limb
- act decisively

Fire

The survival plan
1. first aid
2. *fire*
3. shelter
4. signals
5. water
6. food

In this chapter you will learn why fire is important in survival. You will also learn how to start, maintain, and utilise a safe and effective survival fire. Develop fire-making skills. In fact, fire making is the only survival skill that I ask you to develop and practice. If you simply cannot practice fire starting then give this chapter extraordinary attention.

If you are ever subjected to survival conditions you will be thankful that you learned how to start a fire – especially in wet conditions. There is no challenge in starting a fire in dry conditions. Almost any dead dry material in the woods will burn readily. However, most survival situations occur in adverse weather conditions. Wait until the woods are wet, and then practice fire starting.

Why is fire so important in the survival plan?

The first five items in the survival pattern are first aid, fire, shelter, signals, and water. *These items are often accomplished simultaneously by simply starting a fire.* Exposure or hypothermia is the single biggest cause of death in survival. Survivors do not die of hypothermia in front of an adequate fire! The importance of quickly starting and faithfully maintaining a fire in survival cannot be over-stressed. I once stood in the rain for several hours in front of a fire. I was demonstrating to fellow survival instructors that you needed only a fire to stay warm and dry. My impersonation of a chicken on a rotisserie kept me warm and dry, and thoroughly entertained the other instructors.

Survival Secrets

> **Survival secret**
>
> Fire is also shelter: it eliminates hypothermia.

Building a survival fire can often accomplish everything on the survival plan except food. The survival fire:
- prevents hypothermia
- can be used to melt snow for drinking and to boil water for safe consumption
- provides light to see at night
- produces heat which conserves your energy
- provides a smoke signal in the day, and a light signal at night
- wards off predators, pilfering rodents, and insects
- dries clothing, equipment, fuel and food
- can be used to cook and preserve food

If you cannot build a fire ...

It should now be apparent that fire is an extremely important consideration in many survival situations. If you are ever in a survival situation without the capability of starting and maintaining an adequate survival fire you will have to take extraordinary measures to protect yourself from losing body heat. There are some survival situations where fire is impractical or impossible. You could encounter these conditions on water, in the arctic, in the mountains or on barren land. If you cannot have a fire you should immediately heed the next survival secret.

> **Survival secret**
>
> If you can't make a fire, then your body heat is your fire! Protect it!

The psychological benefits of a survival fire

Fire has many psychological benefits in survival. Fire provides vital companionship. There is a secure comfort zone created around a survival fire that pushes back the wilderness and dispels anxiety. Reducing anxiety will boost your ability to recognise and solve survival problems. Every survival situation will have some unique problems that no amount of training can predict or specifically target. To muster the necessary ingenuity required to solve your unique problems, you must be able to think clearly and to reason effectively.

> **Survival secret**
>
> Fire does far more than just protect you from hypothermia: fire boosts your morale and provides company, security, and control.

Maintaining a fire is valuable therapy. The constant maintenance routine that is required to sustain a fire provides a much-needed sense of purpose. This routine prevents the onset of lethargy, boredom, and loneliness. Keeping active is the secret to remaining constantly alert to rescue opportunities.

By doing nothing more than building a fire, you psychologically and physically establish your territory. Without a fire, one patch of bush is pretty much indistinguishable from the next. The light and smoke produced by your fire are excellent signals. Search and rescue efforts will be specifically looking for evidence of a fire. Fires in the wilderness are generally investigated. This is done not only for forest management considerations, but also because of our basic inquisitive and social nature. Without a fire you must use significantly more effort to be seen and rescued. Without effective signals, you are pretty much invisible in the wilderness.

Fire starting

Effective fire starting requires just a few key ingredients and a little understanding. This book cannot adequately prepare you by simply recommending and describing fire making procedures. You really should get some practical experience in gathering suitable combustible materials and in selecting and preparing a safe, suitable site. You should also practice lighting and maintaining the survival fire. With a little practice and experience you will be able to reliably ignite and maintain a survival fire.

Survival fire requirements

A recommended bush survival fire requires the following ingredients:
1. **tinder:** Thin shavings cut from kindling
2. **kindling:** Split from short lengths, broken from dry dead wood
3. **fuel:** Small standing dead trees are dry and can be easily pushed over
4. **heat:** Matches, lighter, flint and steel, battery, friction, magnifying glass
5. **air:** Arrange both kindling and fuel so that air can enter at the bottom

The most reliable source of fuel in the bush is a standing dead tree. No matter how wet the weather, a standing dead tree will provide you with dry fuel, kindling and tinder. In dry conditions, simply gather any available dry twigs, grass, or leaves to start your survival fire. Birch bark ignites readily even when wet.

Feather sticks

Effective feather-stick fire making can prove to be your most valuable skill in survival. This is particularly true in wet weather.

Split pieces of kindling from a short length of knot free (preferably straight grained) dry, standing dead wood. The pieces should be approximately the thickness of your thumb. Split the wood lengthways by hitting the back of your knife with another piece of wood. Then slice the kindling into shavings or feathers.

Constantly adjust the angle of your blade so that it shaves rather than splits the wood. It takes only a small amount of practice to consistently produce a thin feather. An outward and downward twist of the knife will cause the feather to stick outwards and make room for the next feather. This also provides a visible stopping place for the next feather (see #4 on the next page). Try to leave the feathers attached to the stick.

Turn the stick as required to present a narrow edge whenever the feathers become too wide for easy cutting. Try to prevent the knife from biting too deeply into the kindling. Cutting too deep produces thick feathers that do not curl. They do not ignite or burn easily and are very difficult to cut, requiring significant hand and wrist pressure. Cutting thick feathers causes fatigue, blisters, bruised flesh, and discouragement.

Knives of the multi-tool variety tend to have projections or sharp handle edges. These harsh edges tend to blister or bruise your hands when making feather sticks. You can protect your hands by wrapping the knife handle with cord, cloth, plastic, tape, grass, pliable roots or bark strips.

If you are going to practice outdoor skills in preparation for survival, include feather sticks. You cannot learn to perform a skill quickly unless you first learn to perform the task slowly and accurately. If you begin by cutting feathers very slowly you will train your memory muscles and imprint the correct procedure.

The finished feather stick, when combined with several other feather sticks in a pile, provides the tinder, kindling and initial small fuel to start your survival fire. The ignition flame quickly and reliably spreads from tinder to kindling to fuel.

Additional kindling should then be added to the fire until there is enough fire and coals to support larger fuel.

Mastering this method will ensure a successful fire on your first attempt in a survival situation. Remember to use this method to make all your campfires. You will quickly learn to appreciate and rely upon this technique.

Splitting kindling and making feather sticks

1. Split piece of dead tree

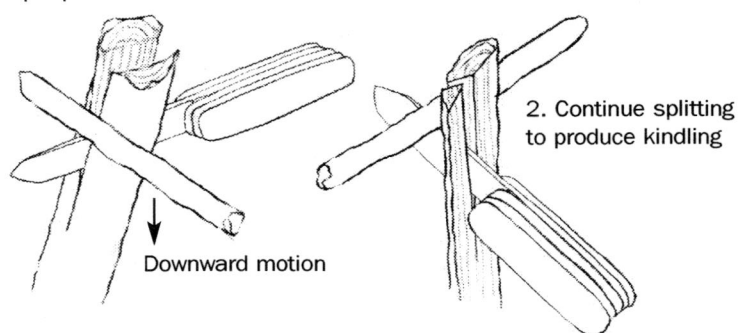

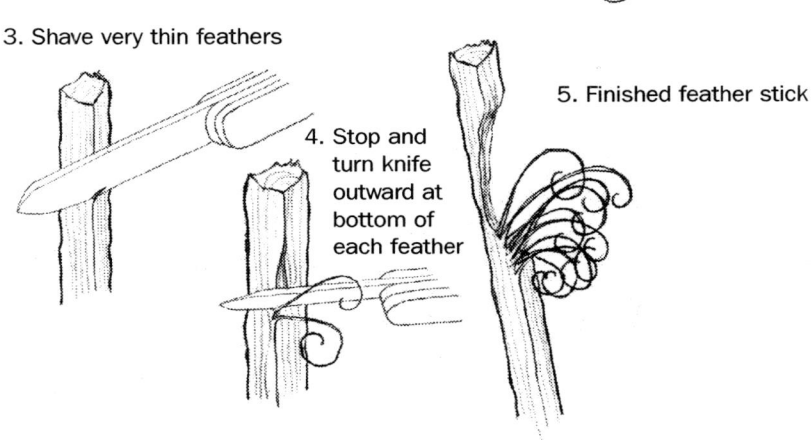

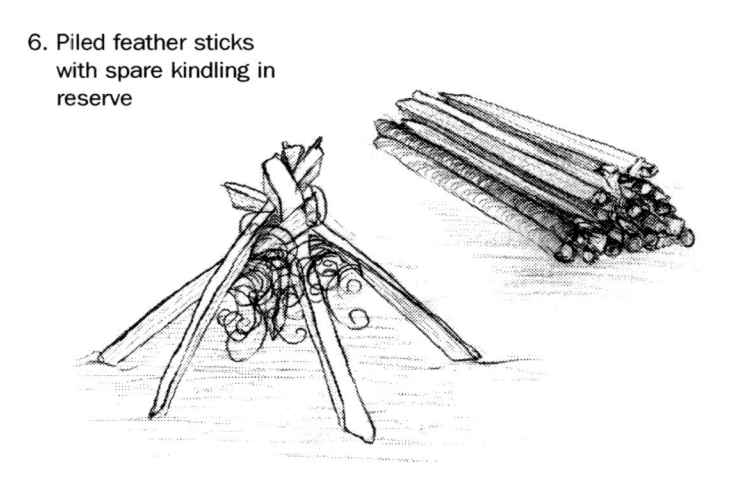

Downward motion

2. Continue splitting to produce kindling

3. Shave very thin feathers

4. Stop and turn knife outward at bottom of each feather

5. Finished feather stick

6. Piled feather sticks with spare kindling in reserve

> **Survival secret**
>
> All you need is a knife and matches.

A tribute to feather sticks

Immediate fire lighting success is psychologically important. The following story illustrates the importance and effectiveness of feather sticks.

A Canadian survival instructor was invited to participate in a survival course given by the British military. The training was purposely conducted on the moors, where the weather was predictably wet and miserable. Even though the students were provided with matches, none had ever succeeded in making a fire.

Undaunted, my friend found a small dead tree that he managed to break up and split into kindling. He then made feather sticks. To the amazement and delight of his companions they were soon huddled around a small but cozy fire that warmed them and enabled them to dry out additional fuel. They kept that fire burning throughout the night.

The object of this particular exercise was to demoralise and to exhaust the students prior to scheduled capture and interrogation. A cold, wet, miserable night on the moors was always effective in achieving this aim. The students' resulting debilitated condition enabled the staff to demonstrate a realistic and effective interrogation without having to use excessive violence.

The next morning my friend's group was captured. Morale was sky-high and the subsequent interrogations were a complete failure. In acknowledgement and tribute to the power of the feather stick, all future students were sent into the exercise without matches!

> **Survival secret**
>
> Practice feather sticks.

You can easily obtain fuel, kindling and tinder for a survival fire using only a knife. Here is a review of the technique.
1. push or break down a small standing dead tree (dead wood is brittle)
2. use leverage to break the dead tree into short pieces
3. split a short length into thumb size kindling with a knife and a chunk of wood as a hammer
4. shave kindling into feather sticks
5. arrange feather sticks, and light at the bottom of the pile

Gathering firewood

36 **Survival Secrets**

Often, at first glance, all standing trees look alive. Closer scrutiny will usually reveal standing dead trees. You will rarely have to travel very far to find standing dead wood in a coniferous or evergreen forest.

The Boreal Forest comprises the bulk of the forested wilderness areas in the Northern Hemisphere. The standing dead wood in these areas is usually softwood. Softwood does not burn for a long time or produce long lasting coals. Dead wood will have lost some of its energy-producing capability due to oxidation through natural deterioration. You will probably require a lot more wood than you might initially suspect. Use your body's stored glycogen energy to gather enough fuel to last through the night (and to accomplish as much of the survival plan as you can!). Remember: if you do not use this stored energy it will be absorbed within 24 hours after you stop eating.

Select a dead tree that is approximately a hand width or smaller in trunk diameter. The reasons for selecting a relatively small dead tree are:
1. they are easy to push down
2. there is less danger of serious injury if a piece breaks off from above
3. they are light, for ease of transporting to your campsite
4. they break into lengths easily when levered between closely spaced trees (see #2 in figure on opposite page)
5. they can be easily split into kindling, using only a knife
6. harvesting small dead trees requires a minimal expenditure of energy

Fallen dead wood is usually plentiful and easy to collect but is often too wet to burn. You can gather wood lying on the ground and pile it behind your fire to dry. This will provide the extra bonus of creating a reflecting wall, which would increase the amount of heat radiated into your shelter. Storing your firewood behind the fire will also keep your campsite uncluttered and safe. As the piled wood dries it may ignite. If this happens simply move it further back.

Survival secret

Maximise your resources and minimise your effort.

Selecting a fire site

It is important to select and prepare a suitable fire site. A wood fire requires a bed of red-hot coals to sustain it. The fire bed must be dry and allow air to penetrate and ventilate the coals at the bottom of the fire. Dry, mineral-based ground is best (i.e. no combustible material).

In deep snow you might not be able to dig down to reach a dry base for your fire. You can make a firebase with "green" or live wood. Green wood will hold red-hot coals, which are necessary to keep a fire burning. Make the green log or branch fire bed several layers thick. The radiating heat from this fire will melt the snow from beneath and around your fire. You will soon have a dry base for the fire and a comfortable dry campsite surrounding the fire area.

Fire site, overhead snow

Snow should be removed from the lower branches of a tree before building a fire.

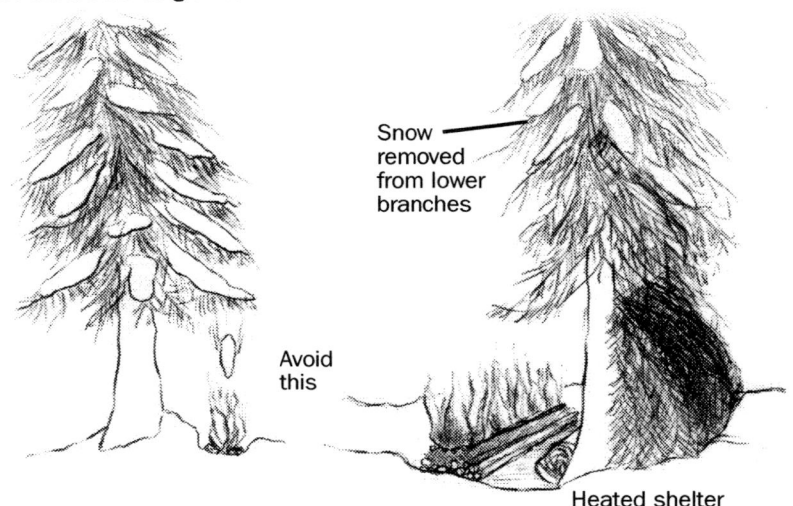

Avoid this

Snow removed from lower branches

Heated shelter

Convection, conduction and radiant heat

Convection heat rises and consequently provides little benefit in a survival situation. Be cautious when starting your fire to ensure that the rising heat does not cause snow from an overhead branch to fall into and destroy your infant fire. Unfortunately people usually try to take advantage of the convection heat rising from the fire to cook or to dry clothing and equipment. People consistently burn critical equipment or food over a fire because of a momentary lapse in monitoring. The loss of burned food or equipment in an actual survival situation is psychologically devastating. Keep items well away from the flame and never directly above the fire.

Conductive heat is transferred by contact from one object to another. A pot uses conductive heat. The fire heats the pot and the pot transfers the heat to the contents. Heated rocks can be placed in a water container to heat or boil the water. Heated rocks also can be used to warm beds. Note: Some rocks contain moisture and can explode when heated.

Radiant heat travels in a straight line in all directions from the fire. Radiant heat can be reflected to increase the efficiency and the effectiveness of your fire. You should use only radiant heat to cook and to safely dry your clothing and equipment.

A commonly taught campfire rule warns: "Don't place your equipment any closer to the fire than you can hold your hand." There is a big problem with this rule. Wood fires fluctuate constantly as the flames rise and subside. A better rule is to warm or dry your clothing and equipment only in your shelter, rather than in front of the fire. If you do set clothing or equipment out to dry near the fire, monitor it closely: watch for sparks or heat fluctuations. When the drying is complete, securely stow the clothing or equipment undercover and well away from heat or sparks.

Convection, conduction and radiant heat

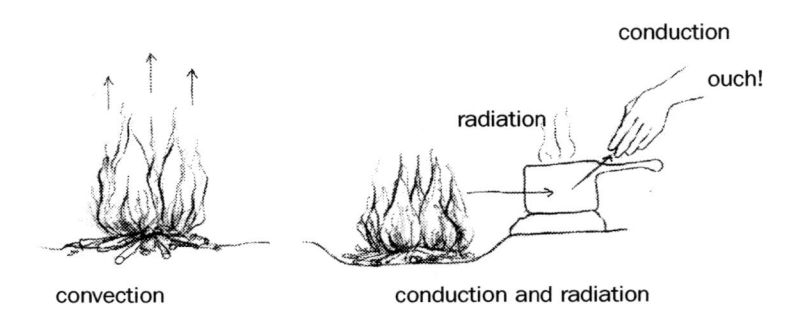

convection

conduction and radiation

Reflecting walls reflect radiant heat

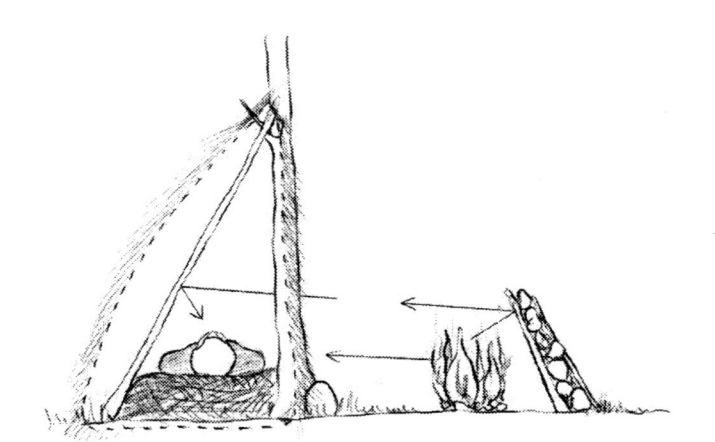

Reflecting wall: making the most of radiant heat

You should build a reflecting wall behind the fire to re-direct radiant heat towards you that would otherwise be lost. The reflecting wall will also act like a chimney and draw the smoke away from you and your shelter. Without a reflecting wall, your body and your lean-to will draw the smoke from the fire towards you!

By understanding radiant energy and taking advantage of its unique properties you can significantly increase comfort and survivability. Because radiant heat energy travels in a straight line, any obstruction between you and the fire will block that energy. Thus, the tradition of digging a fire pit and then surrounding the pit with rocks does not make sense in survival. The reason for digging the traditional campfire pit is to reach below the humus to a non-combustible mineral base. This is a fire safety practice to which I heartily subscribe in non-survival situations. In survival, however, you want an elevated fire to take advantage of radiant heat.

An elevated fire also allows long pieces of fuel to burn into smaller, more manageable lengths. Logs tend to bridge over a fire pit and subsequently stop burning because they are not touching the coals. By elevating your fire you will get the maximum useable energy from your wood. You will conserve fuel and reduce your replenishment requirements, which will conserve your body's energy and extend your survivability.

A circular fire is fine when you are sitting; however, a proper survival fire must be the width of your shelter, so that it warms you equally from head to foot when you lie down.

Body length lean-to plus fire

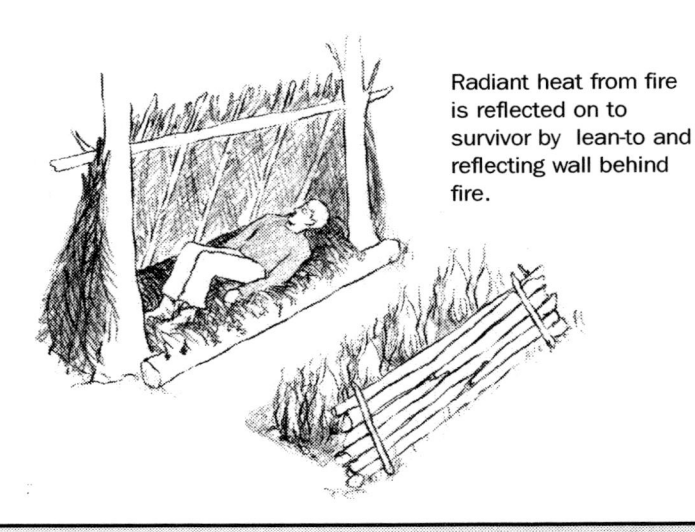

Radiant heat from fire is reflected on to survivor by lean-to and reflecting wall behind fire.

Survival secret

Build a body length lean-to fire when sleeping.

Lighting a fire

Start by placing the smallest fuel (tinder or feather sticks) on the fire bed (ground). Next, place kindling, the thickness of your little finger, on top of the tinder. Make sure you have ample kindling and small pieces of fuel in reserve to continuously feed the infant fire.

Position the flame at the bottom of the material you are attempting to ignite. This will take advantage of all three types of heat (convection, conduction and radiation). Use your body to shield the flame from the wind. Cup your hands around the flame. You want the heat from the flame to travel upwards and spread from the tinder to the kindling. Note: Never pour gasoline on a fire that has already been lit.

Remember: gather enough tinder and fuel before you light the fire and do not leave it until it is well established. If your fire starting fails, do not waste time and matches in a futile attempt to re-ignite the larger remaining pieces of the original fire. It is always better to start from the beginning, this time with adequate amounts of tinder, kindling and fuel.

Survival fire tips

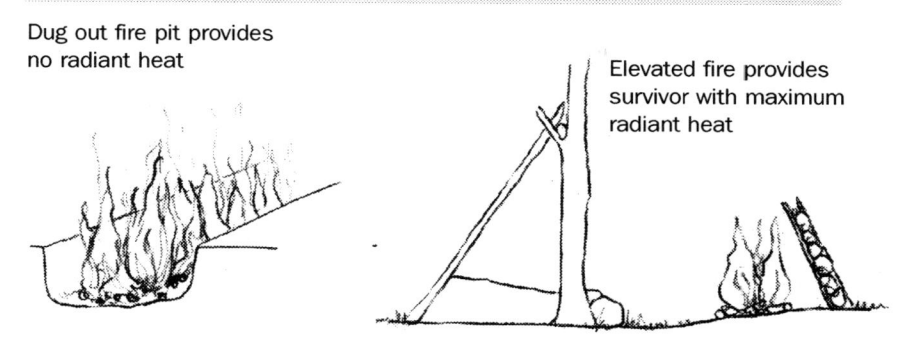

Dug out fire pit provides no radiant heat

Elevated fire provides survivor with maximum radiant heat

Body length lean-to fire

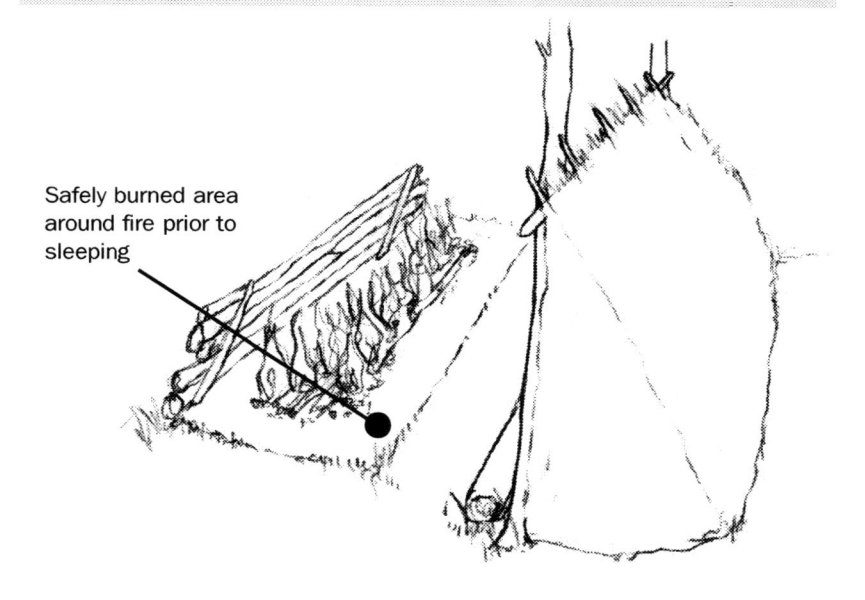

Safely burned area around fire prior to sleeping

Survival Secrets 43

Lighting a fire

Fire set with wind carrying flame up and into fuel

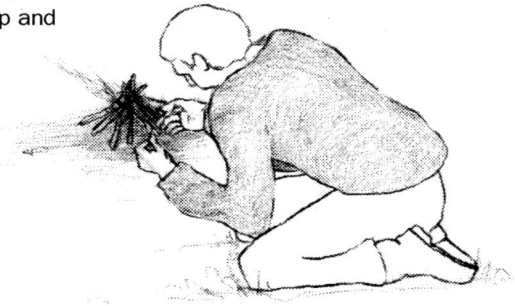

After starting a fire, continually add small amounts of kindling until it has produced some coals. Only when it is burning reliably, with some coals produced, can you begin adding slightly larger pieces of fuel. Once you have large pieces burning reliably, gather an adequate fuel supply. Then prepare and carefully store enough dry tinder and kindling for emergency fire starting. Emergencies include a delayed return to camp from foraging or an extra long sleep. Keep your emergency fire starting material totally protected under shelter, and do not use this material except in an emergency.

Logs on a fire require partners to produce flame. A single log generally smokes and smoulders and does not burn well. Two or more pieces of wood laid close together will cause an upward draft from the hot coals to flow between them. If there are sufficient coals, this hot draft will produce and ignite a combustible gas from the logs. It is this gas that produces flame from a wood fire. The burning gas heats up the wood around it. This heat generates more gas and thus continuously sustains the fire.

You must be vigilant to prevent your fire from burning through combustible ground material and then flaring up in your shelter bed. Build your fire on mineral-based soil if possible or at least on relatively thin topsoil. You can carefully control the burning of combustible ground material around the fire while you are awake. Once all the combustible material around the fire has burned, the fire will stay confined. Ensure an ample safety margin before you lie down to sleep.

Keep the fire going throughout the night for warmth, protection, and signaling. Get most of your sleep during the warmest part of the day. This advice must be considered with the appreciation that search and rescue efforts are concentrated in daylight hours. If you keep well rested and survive passively, you will wake up at the slightest sound of potential rescue.

> **Survival secret**
>
> Sleep during the day in very cold weather.

There is no more pleasant or comfortable survival camp than a lean-to, adequate fire and reflecting wall. You will be amazed at the blissful effect that results from lying on a deep, soft bough bed with heat from your fire radiating upon you from all directions.

Survival review

In a survival situation, a fire will keep you warm, thus saving energy and fending off hypothermia. It will provide light at night and help ward off predators, rodents, and insects. You can use a fire to cook food, boil water (or melt snow or ice), and dry wet clothes. A fire can act as a signal to rescuers. A fire provides companionship and comfort. Maintaining a fire gives you a sense of purpose, and combats boredom and loneliness. Learning how to start a fire and practising the skill, preferably in damp conditions, is critical for survival.

Shelter

The survival plan
1. first aid
2. fire
3. shelter
4. signals
5. water
6. food

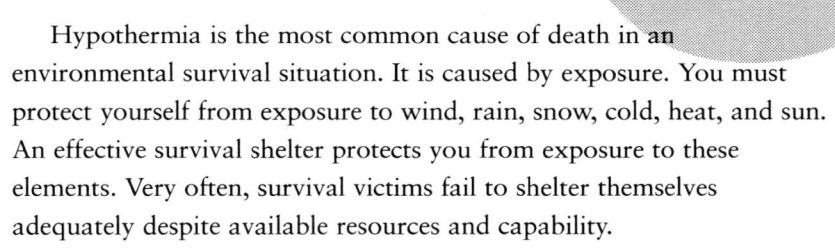

Hypothermia is the most common cause of death in an environmental survival situation. It is caused by exposure. You must protect yourself from exposure to wind, rain, snow, cold, heat, and sun. An effective survival shelter protects you from exposure to these elements. Very often, survival victims fail to shelter themselves adequately despite available resources and capability.

The survival shelter you build will depend on your capability, requirements, and resources. Hypothermia can occur with frightening speed. An effective shelter will preserve both your body heat and your energy reserves. In a harsh environment you must quickly gain protection. The perfect shelter would preserve body heat indefinitely. Even a less than perfect shelter can extend your life from minutes to days. Remember: the object of survival is to extend life one moment longer.

Survival secret

If you have no heat source, then your shelter must minimise heat loss.

The lean-to

The lean-to is one of the best survival shelters. It must be used with a fire. A lean-to can be easily and speedily constructed from a variety of natural or manmade materials. Construction requires no tools.

Lean-to plus fire

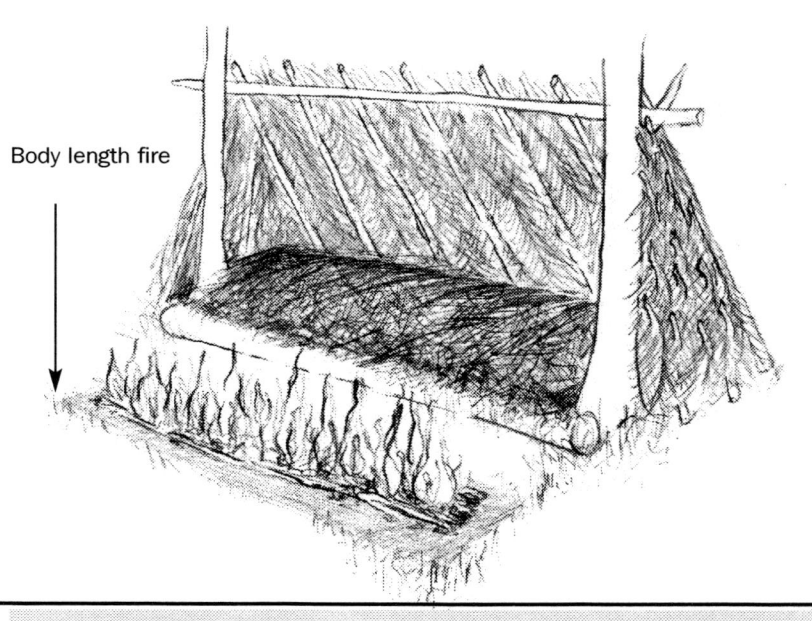

Body length fire

Survival secret

Lean-to plus fire is the best bush shelter.

Shelter site selection

Do not spend an inordinate amount of time searching for the perfect shelter location. Quickly select the best compromise. Completing the survival pattern in a timely manner is paramount. Select your site after assessing your personal capabilities and your surrounding resources. The ideal survival site would be located where you can see and be seen. A view boosts morale, which strengthens the will-to-live.

Safety is paramount. Avoid overhead danger from falling dead trees and branches. Avoid insect infested swamps, low wet ground, gullies, dry streambeds, or potential flood areas. Do not build on large game trails: large predators also use these trails! Avoid obvious rock, snow, or mudslide potential. Weather is often the cause of survival situations and is likely to continue to present problems. Build on high, dry ground. Safe overhangs can provide a quick lean-to by just adding sides.

Availability and proximity of fuel, construction materials, and water is important when selecting a shelter site. Firewood availability is more important than availability of building materials. Building materials only have to be transported once. You need far more fuel than you need shelter material.

Face your shelter towards a ravine or valley if possible. This will provide good rescue visibility, and a nice view, and will keep the prevailing wind across your shelter opening. Wind normally travels up and down a ravine. You want the prevailing wind to blow across the shelter entrance. This maximises protection and minimises smoke irritation. Try to face the opening to the sun to take advantage of daytime heating.

A point projecting out into a lake is highly visible. Almost any wind direction on a point will provide respite from insects. A point on a lake provides easy access for drinking water and is usually a very good location for fishing and netting. Build above the high water indicators, namely driftwood, weed residue and abrupt embankments. Low vegetation is insect habitat, and it should be pulled, cut, trampled, or burned from around the campsite.

Brush lean-to sequence

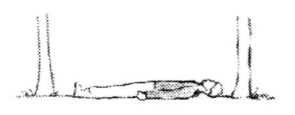

1. Select two trees body length apart plus a little extra length for stowage.

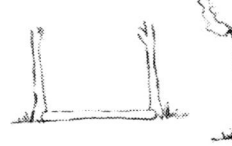

2. Place a comfortable sitting log across the front.

3. Sit on the log and make a mark on each tree slightly above your head.

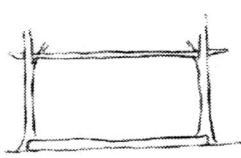

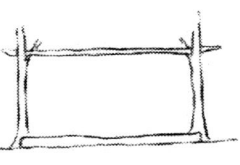

4. Attach a horizontal cross pole on the opposite side of the sitting log at the marked height. You can prop it, tie it or rest it on branches.

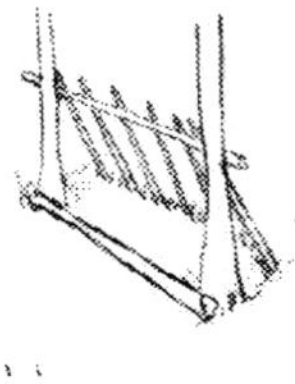

5. Lean several poles against the cross pole. The bottom of each pole should be approximately one and a half times your shoulder width away from the sitting log.

6. Use additional poles to close in each end of the shelter.

7. Layer conifer boughs on the shelter in rows, butt end up, convex or bulging curve out.

8. Start with the bottom row.

9. Lots of boughs will ensure you produce a thick, wind and waterproof, insulated shelter.

10. Fill the bed with boughs until it is thick, warm, dry and comfortable.

50   **Survival Secrets**

Lean-to with tripods

The single person lean-to

You must have an abundant supply of firewood to maintain a body-length fire. A single person lean-to shelter plus fire is designed to provide equal warmth and protection to your entire body. This type of shelter has a slanted roof to the ground, two end walls, and a bed.

The construction of a simple evergreen bough lean-to is shown on the previous page. Dead wood poles are recommended for construction because they are light and easy to harvest, and will not sag. To correctly position the cross pole, sit on the log placed in front of the lean-to and secure the cross pole just slightly above your head. You can use conveniently located branches to support the cross pole or prop it up with a forked pole. You can use rope, twine, roots, or bark to tie the cross pole in place.

Cover the lean-to with layered rows of boughs, starting at the bottom. The butt ends point up and the convex or bulged surface of the bough face out. This overlapping system causes rain and melting snow to run off. The thicker the bough layers, the better the protection and insulation.

The bough bed

You will require a bough bed twice the thickness of your body to ensure warmth, comfort, and dryness. Insulation from the cold ground prevents a great deal of body heat loss. A thick bed will ensure that your sitting log does not block the heat from your fire. A thick bed will also protect you from ground moisture. It is important to keep your body, clothing, equipment, emergency tinder, kindling, and provisions dry. The final advantage of having a deep, soft, dry, insulating bed is comfort. Comfort boosts morale, which is extremely important in your struggle to regain lost control. Sleeping comfortably and soundly also conserves vital energy. Each improvement to your circumstances enhances the possibility of extending life one moment longer.

Bough bed

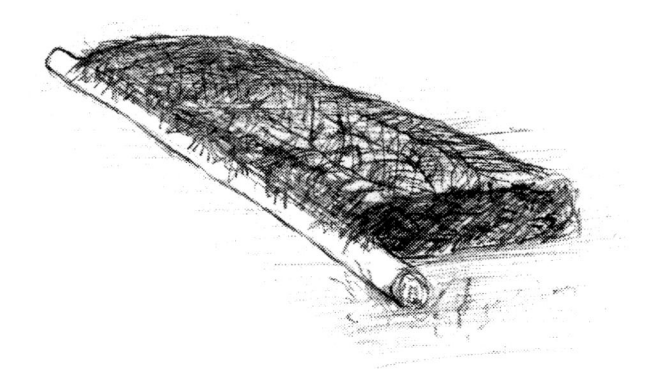

Benefits of a lean-to plus fire
- maintaining a fire keeps you occupied, resourceful, and vigilant
- a fire constantly signals and the lean-to allows you to watch and listen for help. A properly located lean-to and fire is easy to spot by rescuers
- a fire provides company to combat boredom and loneliness
- a fire repels insects, scavengers and predators
- a fire gives light, warmth and allows sleep

- a lean-to and fire makes it easy and convenient to melt snow, boil, cook, purify and preserve food and water while remaining warm and sheltered
- a lean-to and fire safely dries wet clothing and equipment and keeps them dry
- bedding material such as evergreen boughs can be put on the fire to immediately signal rescuers with smoke
- a lean-to is simple, quick, and easy to build. It requires no tools, and uses any available material
- a lean-to provides safe, easy entrance and exit

Snow shelters

Build a snow shelter without tools

You can dig snow caves without tools. You can make snow blocks for an igloo or a simpler shelter with just your hands if the snow is not too hard. In the Arctic you may have to search for recently drifted snow that is soft enough to make blocks with only your hands. You also can push or kick snow into a mound, in order to make a quinsy (pile snow and then dig out a cave).

Snow blocks

Cut snow blocks in the horizontal plane (rather than attempting the vertical or traditional Inuit technique). This method has tremendous advantages in survival. These blocks:

- are easier to cut
- are easier to remove from the hole
- are easier to move into position
- can be made from snow that is not adequate for making traditional vertical blocks
- can be produced with no tools
- do not require lifting or carrying

You can move these blocks into position by pushing with them your head, while you remain down on your hands and knees, protected from the wind.

Simplified igloo construction

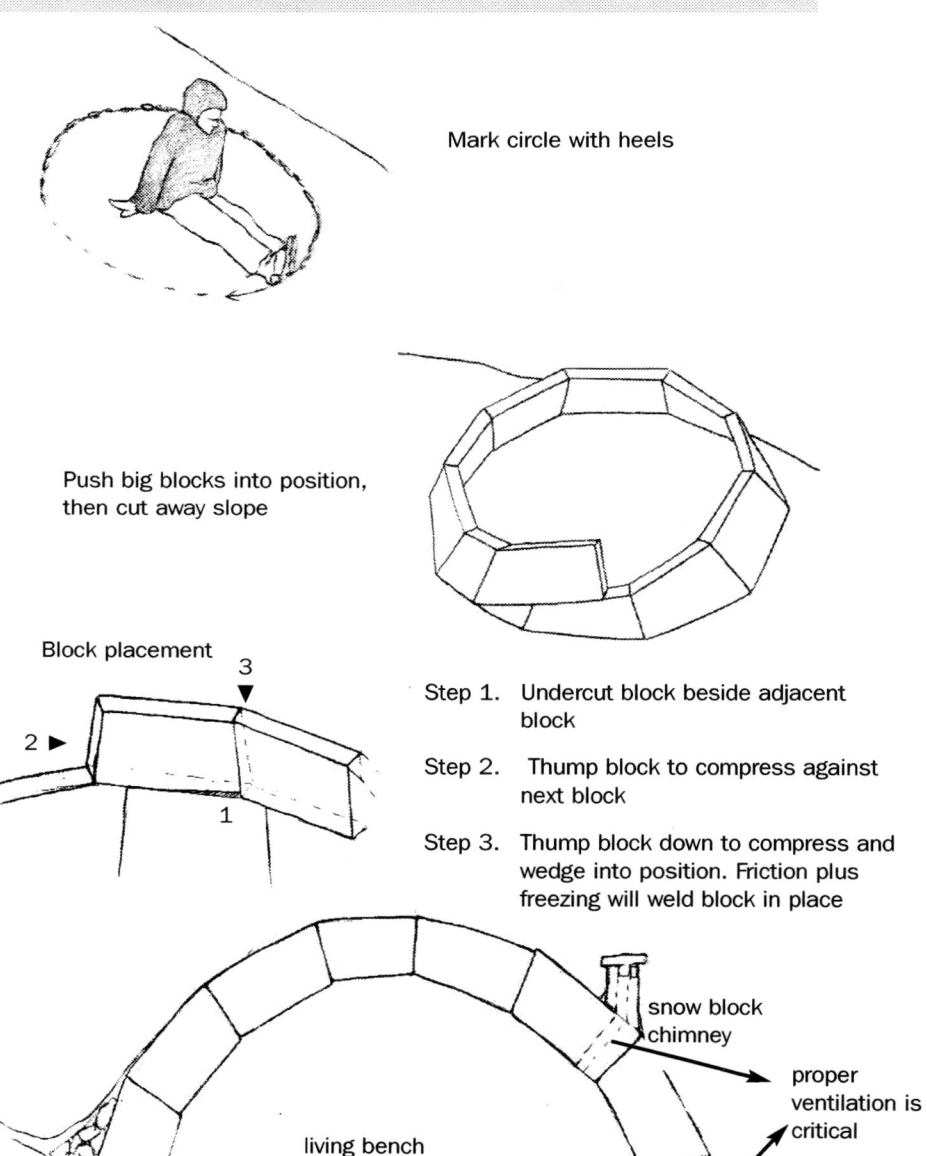

Mark circle with heels

Push big blocks into position, then cut away slope

Block placement

Step 1. Undercut block beside adjacent block

Step 2. Thump block to compress against next block

Step 3. Thump block down to compress and wedge into position. Friction plus freezing will weld block in place

snow block chimney

proper ventilation is critical

living bench

cold well

entrance

cold air

54   Survival Secrets

Making and pushing horizontal snow blocks

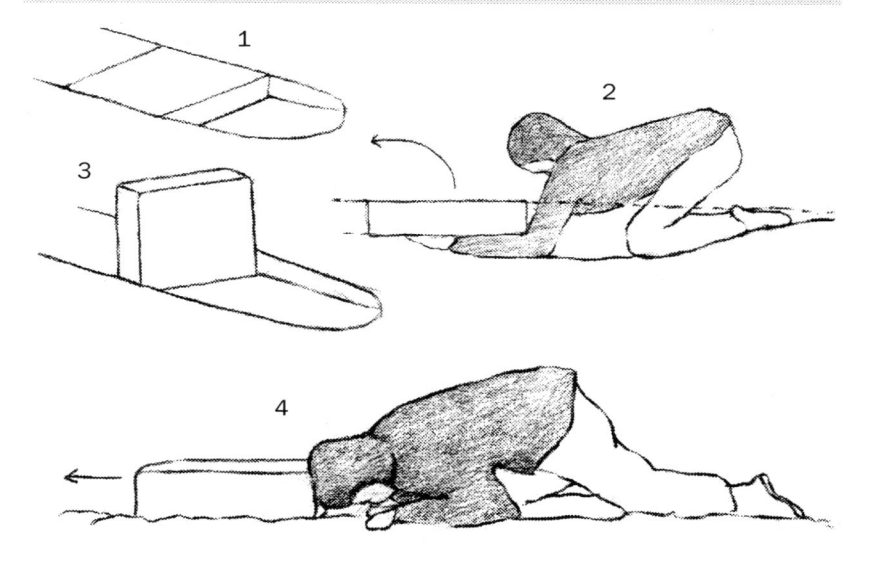

You need only lift on the front a horizontally cut block to rotate it out and on top of the snow. Very large blocks can be cut, levered out of the hole, pushed into position, and finally tilted upright to form the base of the shelter. There is no requirement to lift the block throughout this procedure.

This technique keeps your face and body down and out of the wind. This reduces heat loss and prevents frostbite by protecting your face from the wind and providing a baffle of warm moist breath, which rises back up against your face. Breathing this moist air also reduces dehydration.

The large foundation blocks provide a wide, stable surface to position, manoeuvre, and anchor subsequent blocks. You can complete over half of your igloo by using very large foundation blocks. An injured survivor could use this building method to construct an igloo. My method succeeds with first time builders who are able to construct an igloo quickly and without assistance. Average construction time for first time builders using my training and technique is two hours. (The conventional method requires considerable training and practice and requires 8 to 12 hours for two healthy individuals to complete. Thus, I do not advocate the traditional or Inuit igloo building technique as a viable shelter consideration for inexperienced builders.)

It is not my intention to teach igloo building here. My intention is to demonstrate that innovative survival technique provides alternatives to conventional methods. Survival methods must be simple, easily performed and allow for moderate incapacitation. Otherwise, they are not useful or reliable survival techniques.

Shelters and long-term survival

If your shelter and fire have protected you through the first 24 hours of survival, you can survive for at least the next thirty days if you have sufficient fuel and water. If you are unable to collect large quantities of fuel, you will have to construct a smaller shelter that will keep you warm with a smaller fire.

Ingenuity is an invaluable asset in survival. There are many alternatives in construction material. Materials such as grasses or weeds or bull rushes can be thatched to form shelters. Pieces of sod or moss will work. Enough layers of almost any material will insulate and shed water.

If you are unable to have a fire you may be able to build a huge nest of the warmest driest insulating materials available. You can then crawl in the middle where you will be insulated from all sides. If your shelter does not have a heat source then you must maximise the amount of insulation in your shelter and keep it as dry as possible. Use all the ingenuity you can muster and never accept a bad situation without making every possible effort to improve it.

Completing the survival plan quickly will likely entail some hard work. You must progress quickly to maximise the benefits of your adrenaline and your quick energy reserves or glycogen. Both will be wasted if not promptly utilised. Your aim must be to complete the survival plan quickly then survive passively. Keep it simple and use cunning over effort whenever possible.

Survival secret

Passive survival extends life or, stated another way, the smart, lazy survivor wins.

You should regularly maintain, organise, and improve your shelter and area. A safe, well-organised camp boosts confidence. It is visual confirmation that you are in control. Occupying yourself with camp improvements will avert the devastating effects of boredom and loneliness. You must remain constantly vigilant and prepared to respond instantly to a rescue opportunity.

Nest

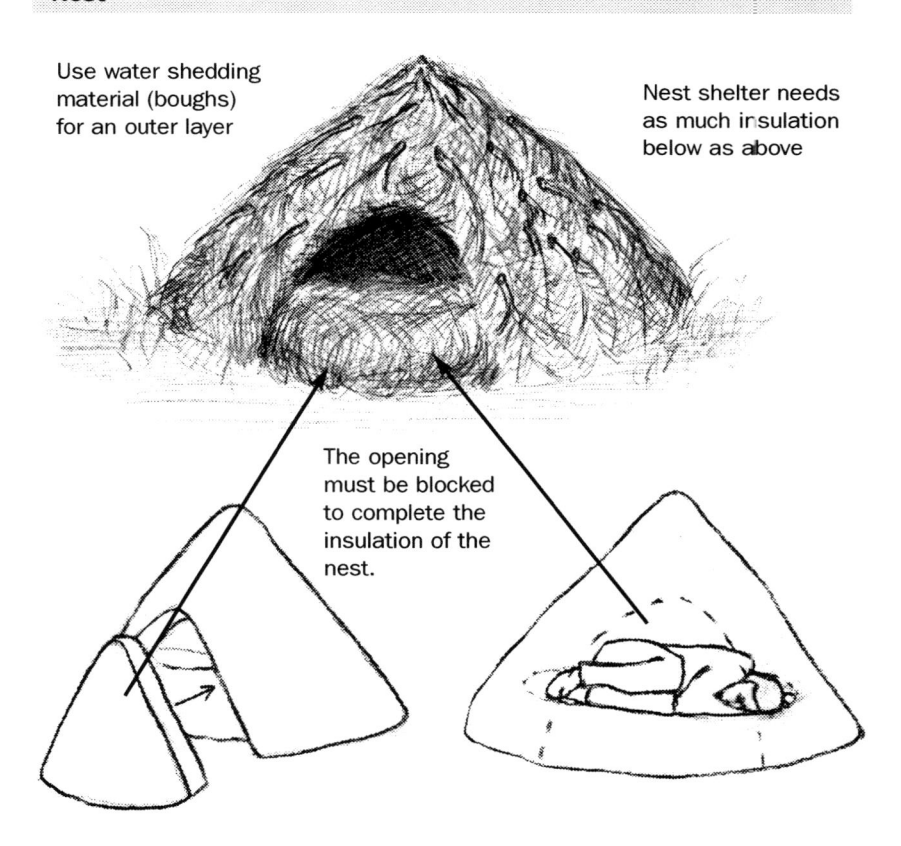

Use water shedding material (boughs) for an outer layer

Nest shelter needs as much insulation below as above

The opening must be blocked to complete the insulation of the nest.

Survival review
- assess your physical capabilities, limitations or injuries
- consider the remaining daylight and the weather. Expect the inevitable interruptions and delays
- assess your need for a fast or small temporary shelter
- assess your requirements for protection from cold, precipitation, wind, insects, or sun
- assess the availability of resources such as fuel, building materials, water, and foraging
- assess safety concerns such as dead trees, loose rock, avalanche, flood, and predators
- consider your orientation with regard to wind, sun, and visibility. A panoramic view boosts morale, and high visibility aids rescue

Signals

The survival plan
1. first aid
2. fire
3. shelter
4. *signals*
5. water
6. food

Effective survival signals speed rescue

Signals are important and often overlooked in survival plans. People in emergency or survival situations are rescued much sooner (and are more likely to survive after rescue) when they signal for help. Satellite communications, locator beacons, and imaging technology have combined to revolutionise search and rescue. Despite technological advances there is a dramatic difference in average rescue time between those who signal and those who don't. This chapter will teach you how to signal effectively so that you can help your rescuers find you.

Survival signals

Note: Three signals of any kind are the internationally recognised distress signal. Try to make three signals equal in size, duration, interval, or distance apart

- **radio:** emergency locator, vehicle or mobile transmitter, and cellular phone
- **light:** vehicle flashers, flashlight, fire, torch, mirror or reflector
- **sound:** vehicle horn, gunshots, whistle, voice, and engine
- **motion:** move a light, wave a flag, splash calm water, and reflect sunlight
- **colour:** bright colors or color that contrasts with the location,
- **shapes:** straight lines, circles, and triangles
- **contrast:** dark against light, light against dark

Survival Secrets 59

- **orientation**: northwest and southeast X on a contrasting background is a signal that can be seen by airborne searchers from any direction.
- **smoke**: light smoke on a dark background and dark smoke on light.
- **location**: visible location such as a hill, clearing, point, shore, or edge of ravine

Saved by a failing signal

Sometimes the world knows that you are in trouble and knows exactly where you are. Despite this knowledge, help is sometimes unable to reach you immediately, because of weather, rescue equipment malfunction, or distance from rescue facilities. I have been personally involved with many search and rescue incidents: let me assure you, searchers depend on signals from survivors.

I recall one particular aircraft crash in the Arctic where signalling saved lives. It was winter in the high Arctic. It was dark twenty-four hours a day. A large aircraft with cargo and passengers had crashed. Almost all of the crew and passengers survived the crash. The weather was initially clear and calm. By the time rescue aircraft arrived overhead blizzard conditions had set in. High winds and poor visibility prevented rescuers from parachuting in to the crash site. Rescue aircraft continuously alternated above the crash site for thirty hours.

The survivors managed to maintain a small fire with salvaged fuel. That fire served as a signal to the rescuers. It indicated that some had survived the crash. The fire eventually began to fail; that failing fire signalled time was quickly running out for the survivors. The airborne rescue personnel immediately decided to disregard the jump restrictions established to protect their safety. They jumped into a black, frigid, windy Arctic void.

The wind was considerably out of jump limits. Thankfully, the rescuers all survived the jump, though some were injured. They somehow managed to save all of the remaining survivors, although the cold had very nearly claimed them. Those in the best condition could have lived only a couple of more hours at best. The fading signal prompted the heroic rescue action that saved many lives.

Search and rescue efforts are often conducted under extremely hazardous conditions. Rescuers routinely put their own lives at great risk while attempting to save the lives of total strangers. It is the absolute moral and civic responsibility of any survivor to minimise the amount of time that these rescuers are exposed to danger.

> **Survival secret**
>
> Effective signaling saves the lives of both survivors and rescuers.

A continuous fire provides a constant signal. Rescuers, forestry officials, and outdoors enthusiasts invariably investigate fires in the wilderness. You can expect a visible wilderness fire to be investigated.

What do rescuers see?

To make an effective visual signal, you should consider your circumstances from the perspective of the person being signalled. Here are some considerations.

Factors affecting signal visibility
- location
- background
- contrast
- movement
- daylight
- back light
- sun or moon position

Evergreen boughs produce white smoke. This provides excellent contrast against a dark forest background. White smoke is less visible against snow. Petroleum products such as rubber, oil, gas, or plastic produce dark smoke. The wood in stumps of trees left from forest fires is high in pitch and produces dark smoke. Dark smoke makes a good contrast against snow.

Try to maintain a constant smoke signal after you spot an aircraft. You should have lots of smoke producing material on hand. Don't be dismayed if you are slow to produce a smoke signal. Airborne rescue

Signals

Three signals in a triangle

Signal smoke must rise above the trees

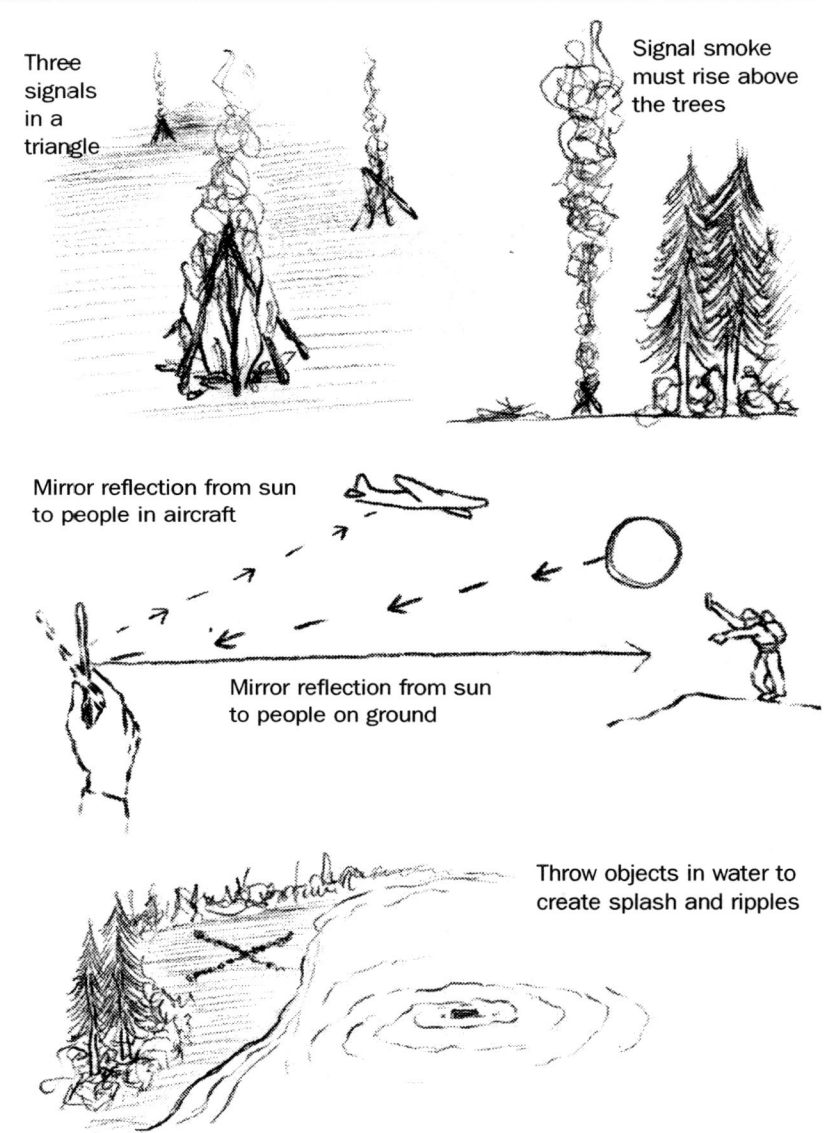

Mirror reflection from sun to people in aircraft

Mirror reflection from sun to people on ground

Throw objects in water to create splash and ripples

spotters are trained to look behind their aircraft for signals from survivors. They realise it takes a while for the smoke signal to rise above the trees. Search and rescue aircraft also use search patterns that enable spotters to see your smoke on subsequent passes. The aircraft will usually return in time to see your smoke signal.

62   Survival Secrets

Keep this thought in mind: Signals that clash with nature attract attention. Here are some ways to make effective signals:
- arrange vegetation in straight lines against a contrasting background
- float dry dead logs. Tie them so that they extend from the shore of a lake or river
- peel or scrape the bark off of green logs, to expose the white inner color, and place them against a dark background
- build a signal fire on a raft on the edge of a lake, pond or river
- cut and arrange snow blocks in a large X pattern with a northeast, southwest orientation. This will produce the maximum shadow effect from all viewing directions
- tramp an X (or cross) in a snow covered clearing, pond, river or lake
- make high contrast circles, lines, triangles or an X by arranging stones, turning up sod, piling brush, heaping snow, cutting snow blocks or spreading ashes from your fire. You can splash calm water with your hands or a pole. You can make ripple rings in water by throwing rocks or wood

A radio or cellular phone in an emergency can speed your rescue if you indicate your precise location. Carry spare batteries. Alkaline or other types of long life batteries have a very long shelf life and much greater reserve, particularly in the cold. Try to keep the batteries warm. The following pictures show some methods of maximising battery life and increasing signal strength.

Snow block and candle and metal reflector

light and heat

metal reflector boosts radio signal

Survival Secrets

Radio inside clothing next to body heat

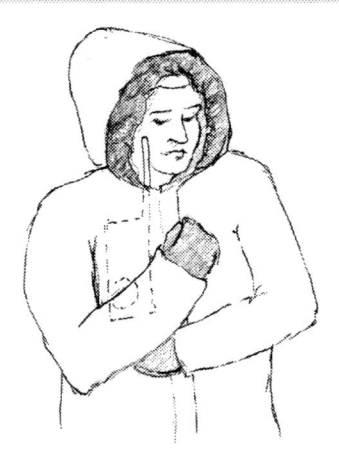

Carry a map and compass even if you have a GPS (Global Positioning System) device. A map will indicate the safest and easiest route to reach safety or simply a better survival location. (A GPS will eventually provide usable topographical information.)

An emergency signal is the most important form of communication you will ever attempt. People normally assume that their communications are understood. This is frequently not the case. In an emergency radio communication, you should repeat what you hear and ask for a confirmation of what you send. Miscommunication in survival may delay or prevent your rescue; the consequences could be fatal.

Survival review

Use all of your ingenuity and available resources to create an effective signal in a survival emergency.

Remember that the internationally recognised emergency signal consists of three of anything. This includes three gunshots, whistles, shouts, light flashes, fires, or any other visual or audible signal.

Make sure that your radio transmission is understood: ask for confirmation of your message and location.

Water

The survival plan
1. first aid
2. fire
3. shelter
4. signals
5. *water*
6. food

The importance of water in survival

Your body is approximately 80% water. Thus I cannot overstress the importance of keeping yourself well hydrated in a survival situation. Failure to maintain hydration, even when water is abundant, is extremely common. The consequences are drastic.

In this chapter you will learn to recognise the signs of dehydration. You also will learn about collecting and conserving water in survival situations.

How long can you live without water?

There is no simple answer to this question. People have been known to die from dehydration in just a few hours. Others have survived for over two weeks without water. The percentage you can afford to lose depends upon variables such as fitness, body fat content, and hydration level prior to the survival situation. Water is far more critical than food in survival.

Dehydration is often self-inflicted. People consistently fail to drink enough in survival even when they have an ample supply. Because most of us are dehydrated most of the time, our bodies have become acclimated to mild dehydration. Unfortunately this means most of us will be dehydrated when our survival ordeal begins.

Thirst and dehydration

Take this simple home thirst test.
1. Drink a litre (quart) bottle of your favourite cola.
2. Then immediately eat a large bag of salt and vinegar potato chips.

Notice how your stomach sloshes and gurgles on the way to the refrigerator for another drink. You are very thirsty but certainly not dehydrated. Similarly, you can be dehydrated and not feel thirsty. Thirst is usually determined primarily by how your mouth feels. Your mouth is often a poor indicator of what your body needs.

When I first began teaching survival I noticed something peculiar. After a couple of days in the field, survival students often complained of illness or simply looked as if they had lost their best friend. Most often, I discovered that the culprit was dehydration.

Symptoms of dehydration can be easily detected. You should constantly monitor yourself for the following symptoms of dehydration:

- dull frontal headache.
- lack of energy
- loss of focus
- loss of willpower
- loss of determination
- loss of ability to reason
- loss of ability to calculate

Familiarise yourself with these symptoms. Test yourself and others regularly in training and in actual survival. Here are three of simple tests you can use on yourself or others:

Test one

Attempt a routine mathematical calculation. Measure your speed and accuracy relative to normal expectations. If a routine calculation is slower or more difficult than normal, you can suspect dehydration (also suspect hypothermia or fatigue).

Test two

Gently pinch the skin on the back of the hand. If the skin remains tented it is an indication of significant dehydration.

Test three

Squeeze the end of a finger and gauge how quickly the colour (blood) returns to the fingertip. (This is my favourite test for dehydration.)

When dehydration is suspected in a survival student I squeeze one of their fingertips. Then we both observe the rate at which the blood flows back into the finger at the base of the fingernail. I then very gently squeeze my own finger to demonstrate how much more quickly I recover. I then insist that the student drink at least a litre (quart) of water at once. (Remember: 85% of us are dehydrated most of the time.)

In almost every case the recovery is miraculous and students are permanently convinced to drink adequately in an actual survival situation! Within five or ten minutes the headache is gone and is replaced by renewed enthusiasm and energy. If symptoms persist, I know that I am dealing with an actual illness as opposed to self-inflicted dehydration.

It rarely occurs to the student that I have squeezed his or her finger harder than my own to guarantee the appearance of dehydration. If they do become suspicious, I then know that their mind is still functioning perceptively. These students would not likely be significantly dehydrated. So far no student has questioned this test. (By revealing my secrets and tricks in this book I will be forced to invent new techniques!)

How you lose water in survival

You may lose water through:
- bleeding (internal and external)
- burns
- nausea
- diarrhea
- urination
- perspiration
- respiration
- metabolism
- digestion
- exposure (sun, wind, heat)

Bleeding, both internally and externally, can cause significant dehydration. Most hunters are aware that a wounded animal may lose large amounts of blood internally. They sometimes cannot be tracked because they do not leave a significant blood trail; however, they can be located by scouting near water. Significant blood loss results in severe dehydration, which causes a raging thirst.

Injury is often the major contributor to dehydration in survival. Your group may have a limited supply of water. You must give injured survivors the water they require. Remember: survival means extending life one moment longer. Giving your limited water to the injured will not significantly shorten your life. When you go without water, your body becomes progressively more water retentive and uses its dwindling supply incredibly efficiently. Try to drink enough to maintain minimum acceptable hydration levels in order to maximise your cognitive and physical capabilities as long as possible. Thus you will remain more alert to the possibility of rescue and to inventing ways to improve your situation.

It is important to sustain your ability to help yourself and assist rescue efforts. If you do not have an adequate supply of water, you must make every effort to minimise your dehydration rate.

Survival secret

Do not ration water.

Water quality and safety

Not all water is consumable (potable). Nature attempts to purify water using sunlight and oxygen as antibacterial agents. You can add iodine, bleach (chlorine), or commercial purification tablets to partially purify water, but only boiling will kill Giardia, the cause of beaver fever, and other harmful organisms. Boil water for at least ten minutes, particularly when you are well above sea level. In cases where you are unable to purify water, running water is a safer choice than stagnant water. (Stagnant water can be dirty, foul smelling, horrible tasting and unsafe to drink. A hole dug beside stagnant water will normally fill with clearer, safer, better tasting water.)

There are reverse osmosis filters on the market that remove salt, bacteria, parasites, and chemicals. They are light, compact and, I hope, already in all life rafts. Drinking seawater will cause you unimaginable suffering and hasten your death.

> **Survival secret**
>
> Do not drink seawater!

People are often reluctant to drink water directly from nature. It sometimes contains debris and may have an unpleasant taste or odour. Filtering water through sand, grass, moss, cloth, or charcoal that has been smothered by ashes in your campfire will not make water safe, but it will improve its look, taste and smell. Improving the taste of water is very important. It will encourage people to drink adequately. If necessary, hold your nose when you drink to reduce the obnoxious taste and smell of the water.

People do not usually like the flat taste of boiled water. Shaking or pouring boiled water from one container to another will replace lost oxygen and will significantly improve the flavour. Do the same for water from melted snow or ice. It will improve the flavour.

A delicate subject

Urination and excretion both cause you to lose water. A healthy well-hydrated adult will produce a minimum of two litres of urine per twenty-four hour period. Many survivors become very concerned when they notice that they continue to urinate even when they have had nothing to drink. Urine is a necessary by-product of your basic metabolic functions. Knowing this will prevent you from worrying needlessly or becoming stubbornly retentive. If you are properly hydrated, your urine will be clear and almost colourless.

The relative merits of urine consumption in survival can be reduced to the following advice: do not do it. Urine consumption will not measurably forestall dehydration or extend your life. You require several litres of water daily to maintain normal hydration levels. The very first, relatively dilute, urine specimens are in fact drinkable (potable), but they total less than two litres. Thus they are not sufficient in themselves to re-hydrate you and drinking them would not extend your survivability significantly. In a water limited survival situation, you are better advised to focus on reducing moisture loss. Reducing moisture loss is the best way to extend life one moment longer.

Simple water gathering techniques

Some simple water gathering techniques require very little effort. You can wrap transparent plastic around foliage. As the plant transpires, it will expel water vapour, which will condense on the inside of the plastic. Place a weight inside the plastic and the water will gather at the low spot created by the weight. Cut a hole at this point to collect the water. The hole can be tied shut and more water gathered until the plant's moisture has been depleted. You can then harvest water from another plant.

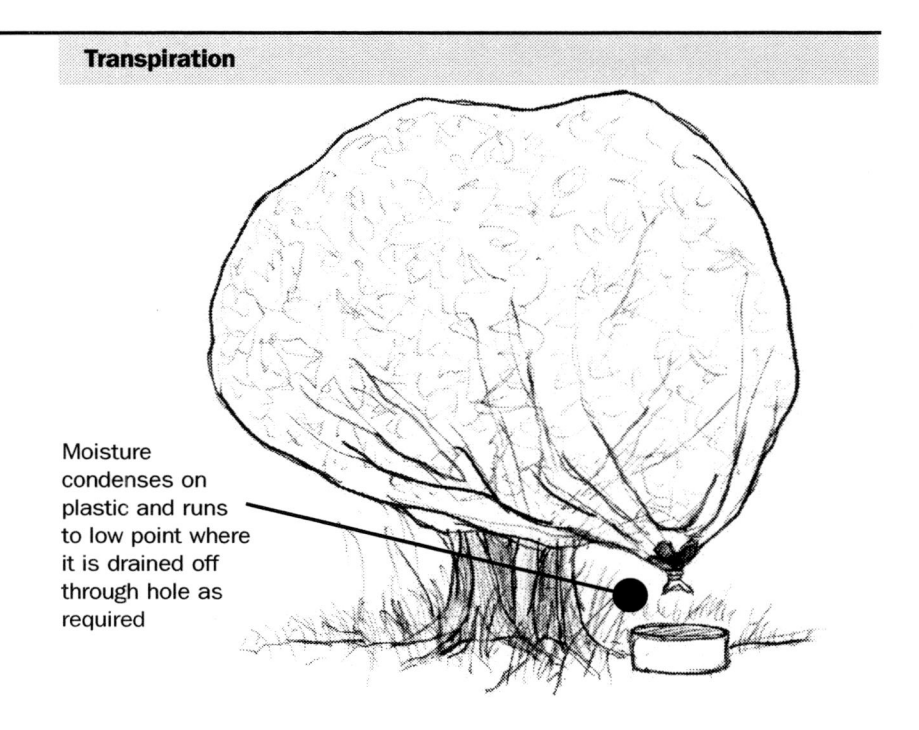

Transpiration

Moisture condenses on plastic and runs to low point where it is drained off through hole as required

Dew

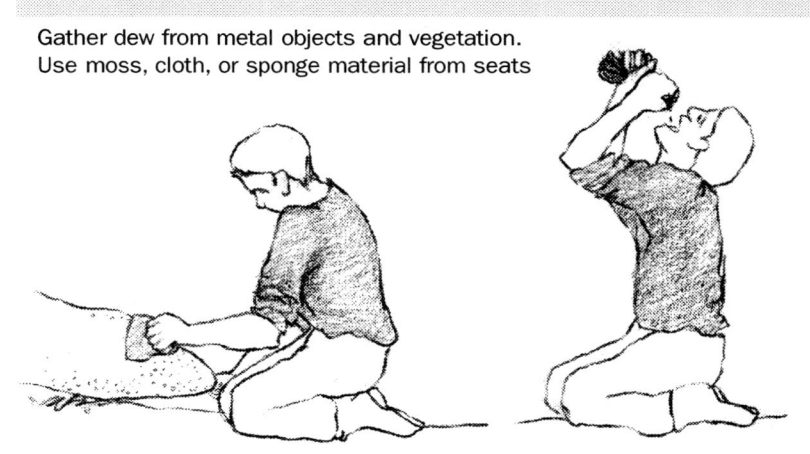

Gather dew from metal objects and vegetation. Use moss, cloth, or sponge material from seats

Another easy water gathering technique is to absorb dew from plants and other surfaces with cloth or moss or any other absorbent material. You can then wring the water from the material.

In arid climates, watch for places where wildlife gets water. Green vegetation may indicate water sources. Depressions in outside bends of dry riverbeds can sometimes hold water just below the surface. The water from wet mud can be squeezed out or you can use clear plastic to extract the water by evaporation and condensation.

Water supply discovered by observing wildlife

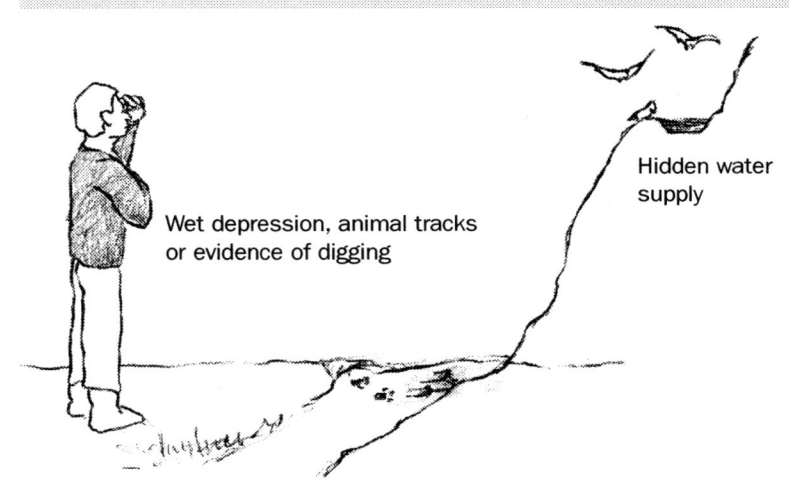

Hidden water supply

Wet depression, animal tracks or evidence of digging

Survival Secrets

Dry riverbed water source

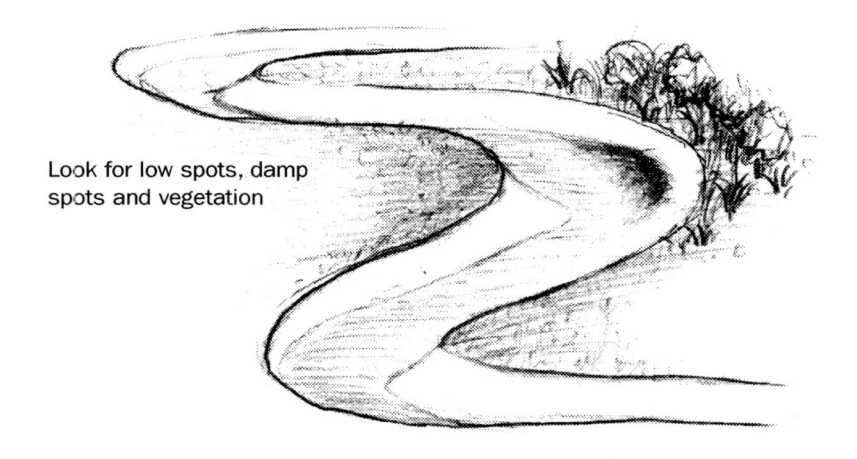

Look for low spots, damp spots and vegetation

You should constantly seek to innovate in survival. The effect of one small improvement might appear insignificant, but the cumulative benefit of many small improvements can be substantial. There are always psychological benefits derived from attempting any improvement. Doing something proactive in survival effectively nurtures the will-to-live. These efforts will help extend life "one moment longer."

Reducing water loss

Sometimes you risk losing more water through perspiration than your efforts return, even if you are successful in obtaining some water. In some situations minimising water loss is your best course of action. Here are some ways to minimise water loss:

- **first aid:** The timely application of first aid will help minimise dehydration, particularly in the case of bleeding and burns
- **protection:** Protection from sun and wind and heat reduces dehydration. Desert dwellers keep covered in the sun and heat
- **do not eat:** You need water to digest food. You can live a lot longer without food than without water. If you are in a water-limited survival situation, do not use diuretics such as tea or coffee

- **survive passively**: Avoid unnecessary physical activity. Try to perform your chores in the early morning or evening when it is cooler. In desert conditions try to get above or below the ground to minimise the effects of daytime heat

You can even reduce the rate of dehydration caused by breathing. When you breathe in, your lungs moisten the air to approximately 85% humidity. That moisture is lost when you exhale. In dry and particularly cold dry climates the relative humidity is below 10%. You can lose more than four litres (a gallon) of water per day from breathing.

To reduce dehydration in frigid dry conditions, cover your mouth and nose with a scarf or other material. This will create a warm, moist buffer. The material will hold some of the expelled heat and water vapour. When you inhale, you will recapture some of the trapped moisture and heat. Covering your face will also prevent frostbite.

Concentrating on ways you can reduce your moisture loss will help you focus on survival issues rather than your thirst. Keep a button or small rock in your mouth to stimulate salivation.

Motion sickness and dehydration

Motion sickness is very common in life rafts. Unfortunately, some bureaucracies have eliminated motion sickness medication from life rafts. If you have motion-sickness medication, take it as soon as possible to maximise effectiveness. Vomiting causes rapid and severe dehydration. Motion sickness is also extremely demoralising: it significantly reduces your motivation to effect improvements, to signal, or to look for rescue. Motion sickness severely diminishes the will-to-live.

Survival review

In a survival situation, if you have ample water, drink frequently without waiting for thirst to prompt the initiative. Do not ration water.

If you do not have ample water, concentrate on ways to reduce moisture loss: apply necessary first aid; protect yourself from the elements; do not eat; survive passively; and, if you are on the water, take motion sickness medication to prevent vomiting. You must give injured survivors the water they require.

The following two survival situations illustrate the importance of staying hydrated.

Dehydration can kill quickly

Two women were driving through the American desert. They turned off the highway down a dirt road to visit a friend. They drove a couple of miles until they realised they were on the wrong road. When they attempted to turn around the car became stuck in the sand. The driver told her friend to remain in the air-conditioned comfort of the vehicle while she walked back to the highway to flag down help.

The driver was soon perspiring heavily in the hot sun. She was considerably overweight, which meant her critical weight loss threshold due to moisture loss was significantly lowered. She collapsed when she reached the highway. A passing motorist notified an ambulance service immediately. The woman did not survive the trip to the hospital. She died from the effects or complications brought on by dehydration within just a couple of hours.

Students usually guess quite accurately at the maximum time you can survive without water. However, people are not aware that in extreme conditions the survival time can be as short as just a couple of hours! Lack or loss of water can have a devastating impact on your survivability in an incredibly short space of time. It is helpful to understand how factors combine to extend or shorten your life expectancy in an environmental survival situation.

In a hot, dry, hostile environment, without water, you must take precautions to reduce dehydration. Failing to do this can reduce your survival time to a matter of hours. You can extend your life significantly by taking cover from the sun and wind and covering your skin. These actions will reduce moisture loss due to perspiration and evaporation. You should also avoid physical activity during the heat of the day.

Minimising dehydration

A man was cast adrift on a one-person life raft following a mishap at sea. The temperatures were warm both day and night. He had no water and knew that he could not drink the salt seawater. He remained passive to minimise his moisture and energy loss. He kept himself covered to prevent injury and dehydration from the sun. He had some food but chose not to eat it because he knew that without water the food would dehydrate him further. He was aware that he was in greater danger from dehydration than starvation.

The man kept a button from his clothing in his mouth to avoid the torment of thirst as long as possible. He initially took seasickness medication to combat the nausea and vomiting that is so prevalent in life raft situations.

This survivor applied knowledge, experience, and ingenuity to maximise his survivability. He was rescued and successfully revived after ten days at sea without a drop of water to drink. Uninjured survivors, in a warm moist environment, have survived for ten days to two weeks without water.

Food

The survival plan
1. first aid
2. fire
3. shelter
4. signals
5. water
6. *food*

Hunger and survival

Hunger is much easier to deal with than any other survival discomfort. Most people do not need food for at least thirty days. When you stop eating your digestive system shuts down. As long as it remains shut down, you'll feel no discomfort. When you think about food you activate the digestive system, and it starts up in anticipation of receiving food. Concentrate on other survival matters. Do not think or talk about food.

How long can you live without food?

Most people have enough stored energy in their body to survive without eating for at least thirty days. Also note that you will not suffer serious consequences due to the lack of vitamins, trace elements, and minerals during that amount of time. The average adult uses between 1,800 and 2,200 calories daily. The number of calories you consume depends upon your size, gender, fitness, and level of activity. Most of your stored energy is fat. Humans normally have more than 10% body fat. A trim (10% body fat) individual, weighing 100 kilograms, would have 10 kilograms of fat. Fat has 9 calories per gram. This person would have 90,000 calories available. If you divide 90,000 by 2,000 you will discover that this person has at least a 45-day energy reserve. Clearly, lack of water will cause your death before lack of food.

Humans evolved from a tropical climate and are well protected from over-heating. We fail miserably when it comes to heat production and retention in cold weather. In order to use our abundant body fat as fuel, we must first convert it to sugar. This is a slow and complicated process. It consumes our muscle tissue as well as our fat. It also requires water, which is often scarce in a survival situation.

> Remember to take full advantage of your body's stored glycogen or quick energy. Complete the survival pattern as quickly as possible. Your body will metabolise your glycogen within the first twenty-four hours after you stop eating. Use it because you cannot save it.

To eat or not to eat ...

Of all the nutrients contained in food, simple carbohydrates (sugars) such as those contained in sweet candies are the most quickly and efficiently digested. They are more water-saving than any other food. Remember: digestion requires water, and, in survival, you should be much more concerned about lack of water than lack of food. However, in some extreme cold survival situations, you might consider eating simple carbohydrates even if you do not have any water. You could use the energy from them to produce body heat when cold threatens your immediate survival.

The next type, complex carbohydrates, are primarily starchy foods like bread, pasta, potatoes, or rice. They are digested easily, quickly, and efficiently and require very little water to digest. Most of the four calories per gram are made available for energy production.

Compared to carbohydrates, protein is harder to digest, uses much more water, and provides less net energy.

Fat has more than twice the energy of any other food, but it requires significant amounts of water to digest. The digestion, assimilation, energy production, and water requirements are the same for fat whether it comes from an animal or vegetable source.

Survival review

In general, I would advise you to refrain from eating in a survival situation if you do not have access to ample amounts of water. You must use a limited supply of water to keep yourself hydrated. You can live a long time without food; you cannot live without water.

Survival secret

In survival the only thing you need from food is energy.

Foraging

chapter 10

Do not consider foraging for food until you have completed the survival plan!

Foraging benefits and dangers

While it is true that the only thing you need from food in survival is energy, there are other benefits to foraging. Harvesting anything edible can boost your morale. Foraging will help prevent boredom and loneliness. It will keep you alert to the prospect of rescue.

Some wild plants have medicinal and therapeutic properties, but you must be sure you know what you are harvesting and how to prepare it. Survival is not the time or place to poison yourself or suffer an allergic reaction. If you don't recognise it, don't eat it!

Many survival books describe both edible and poisonous plants. The identification features of poisonous plants are usually reinforced. Features of poisonous plants therefore tend to be remembered better than those of the edible plants. Without significant field experience to back up the classroom lectures, there is a natural tendency to transpose the poisonous features into the edible category. For this very good reason, I refuse to show slides or describe poisonous plants in basic survival training.

Learn how to safely harvest wild plants but remember the next survival secret.

Survival secret

If you don't recognise it, don't eat it.

Conserve energy by always practising passive survival. Use the survival plan to help you create a foraging checklist. Combine foraging trips for plants, water, fuel, and game.

Foraging checklist

1. **first aid**: are you capable of foraging without risking injury or re-injury?
2. **fire**: how long will the fire burn and is there a safe cache of dry tinder, kindling and fuel?
3. **shelter**: is your shelter safe from the fire (flare up or wind change)?
4. **signal**: will your fire provide a constant signal in your absence for you and your rescuers?
5. **water**: do you have water on route, or available upon your return?
6. **food**: have you made a plan to forage for items in addition to food?

You should always have a reasonable fire burning before leaving your bush campsite to forage. I emphasise reasonable. Returning to a burned out camp is not good for morale and starting a forest fire is not very high on the list of recommended ways to counter boredom and loneliness.

If you sustain an injury, or the weather turns while you are foraging, you will appreciate being greeted by a nice warm fire upon your return to camp. It is easier to add fuel to a fire than to start a new one. Your fire functions as a beacon to guide you back to camp if you become lost or disoriented. This can easily happen if your attention becomes focused on foraging rather than navigating. Your fire is a constant signal for help. You don't want to miss a rescue opportunity while foraging for food you didn't need in the first thirty days.

There are many good reasons to forage close to your camp. Small animals such as rabbits, squirrels, and a variety of birds are likely to live near your camp. (If you don't see evidence of any birds or animals, you may want to re-evaluate your campsite selection.) Many small animals habitually follow the same routes. They make trails that provide excellent opportunities for setting snares. Animals are often active after dark. A snare or trap works for you 24 hours a day.

When humans move through the woods most animal activity ceases. If you sit still, the animals soon recommence their activities. You will be amazed at the amount of wildlife in your vicinity. Observing their activity will keep you alert. It will also provide clues to devising methods for catching them. If you sit and stare dully into the fire it is unlikely you will think of ways to improve your situation. You will descend into an abyss of boredom and loneliness. In wilderness survival situations you are bound to have neighbours. These birds and animals can provide valuable company. This may be more important than sustenance.

> **Dealing with hunger**
>
> Try not to think about food. Anticipation of food will stimulate your digestive system. This is both painful and demoralising. If you keep your mind occupied with something other than food you will not feel as hungry. Keep busy by attempting to improve your situation.

Respect the law of diminishing returns

There are some circumstances where foraging is impractical. In a snow shelter on the Arctic tundra, maintaining body heat would take precedence over foraging, because 90% of all winter life in the Arctic is located within a half mile (less than a kilometre) from an open lead in the ice.

I would not recommend travelling far to forage in the Arctic. Light conditions peculiar to high latitudes and the dry clear air make distances difficult to estimate. Objects on the landscape that appear no more than a kilometre away will turn out to be more than five kilometres away. The law of diminishing returns must be respected when foraging in survival.

Simple weapons and snares

As mentioned, the most effective method to harvest birds, animals and fish is to set snares, traps and nets. You can, however, make a simple, effective and easily used weapon to harvest small ground game. Split one end of a hefty throwing stick, and weight it with a rock that is inserted and lashed. Throw the weapon at a bird or animal on the ground. Make the stick spin horizontally like a helicopter blade. You have a wide margin of acceptable error with this weapon. If the stick lands short it can bounce up and still hit your target. This weapon cuts a wide swath. You should carry this weapon while engaged in activities

Snaring (wire snare)

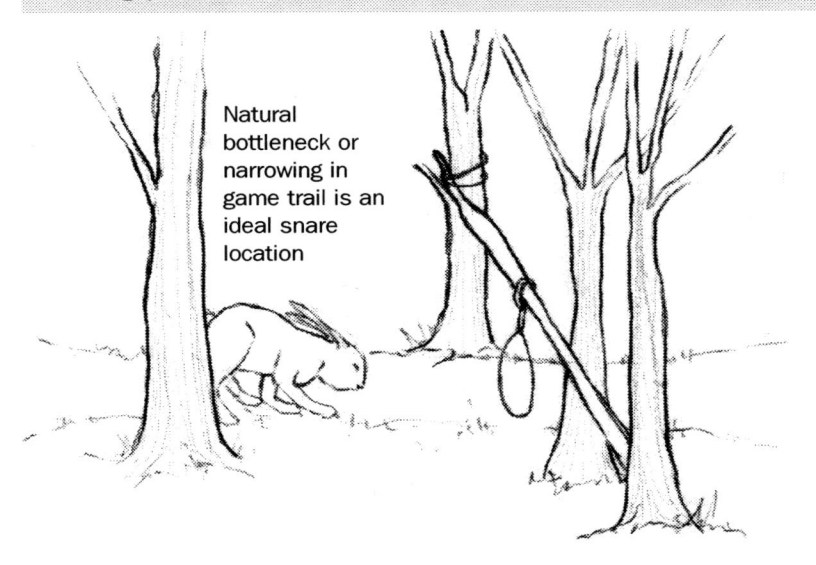

Natural bottleneck or narrowing in game trail is an ideal snare location

Snaring (non-wire snare)

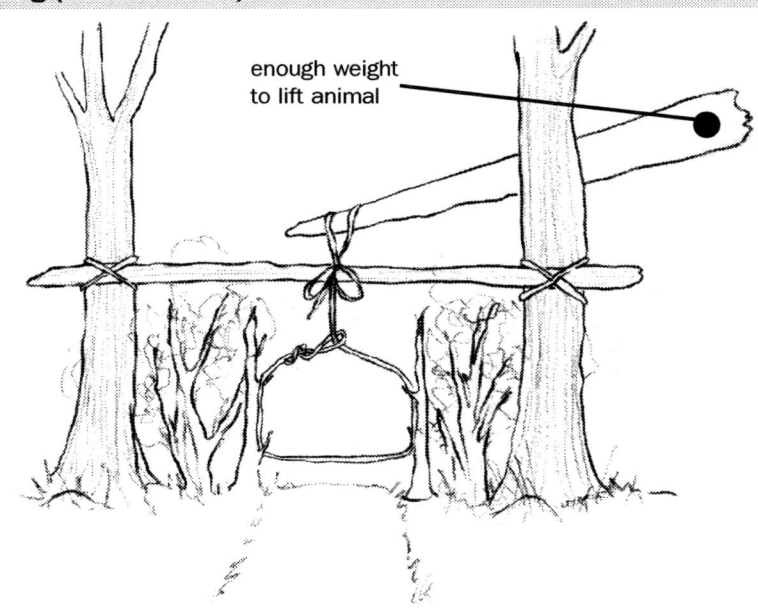

enough weight to lift animal

Survival Secrets

such as getting water or fuel. Remember, passive trapping, netting or snaring is by far the most energy efficient method to forage for game

Snaring is a pretty simple concept:
1. make a slip noose or snare
2. place the snare in the path of an animal
3. the animal gets caught as it travels along the path
4. you eat the animal
5. you reset the snare

You can make snares out of many materials, including wire, twine, or line made from grass or strips of bark. Test the strength and durability before you set the snare. Ensure that the loop closes smoothly and tightly. Make the snare opening roughly twice as big as the head of the animal you are intending to snare. Too big is better than too small. Animals are often successfully caught around the body instead of the neck if the snare is too big. You won't catch anything if the snare is too small.

Remember that it is the bottom of the loop that actually catches the animal. Conventional snare instruction tells you to make a round loop. A better snare employs a loop that is wide across the bottom. Widening the loop at the bottom increases the chances of catching the animal. I challenge the effectiveness of setting conventional rabbit snares four finger-widths above the ground with round loops. My method sets the bottom of the loop only two finger-widths above the ground, with the loop widened at the bottom. I have found this method very effective.

Set the loop across the path of the animal you are hoping to snare and remember to secure the end of the line to something that will hold the animal. It would be very discouraging to watch your dinner on a leash, running through the woods, advertising your ineptitude.

If the snare is not made with wire the animal will simply turn and chew its way to freedom. To prevent this you must attach the snare to a pole or branch that will spring upwards when triggered. Tie the snare to a bent sapling or a counter-weighted pole and make a trigger to hold

Snaring

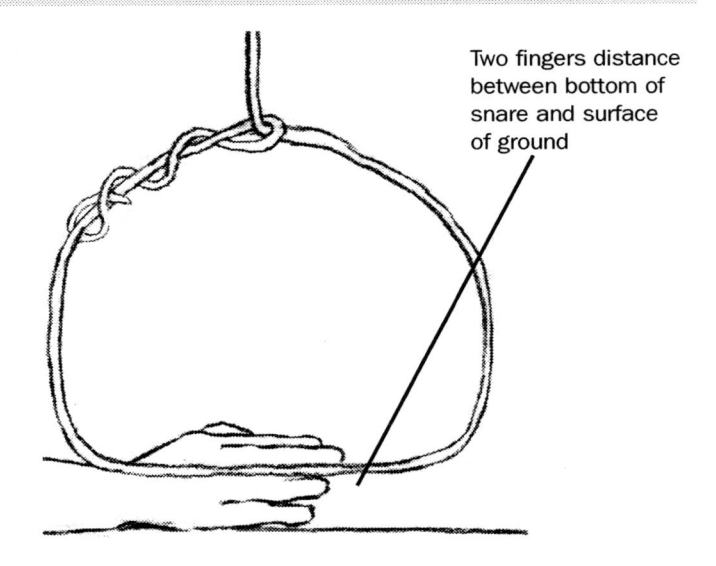

Two fingers distance between bottom of snare and surface of ground

the mechanism down. When the animal pulls the snare tight around its neck, it triggers the release. There are endless methods to accomplish this trick. As a starting point, just remember how a bow ties your shoes securely but comes undone when you pull on the ends. Make your snare so that the snared animal pulls on the knot and releases the mechanism.

Wild animals (except the polar bear) tend to be fearful of human scent. Animals generally travel with their noses close to the ground to detect danger. Avoid leaving your scent on the animal trail and around the snare. Approach the snare site carefully from the side. When setting or checking snares, disturb as little as possible

Make lots of snares, and do not expect to catch an animal in each snare.

There are many outdoor books that go into great detail regarding setting traps, snares, and nets. This is a book about survival essentials, not outdoor living or bush craft. If you don't know or cannot remember how to set a trip snare, you can experiment in front of your fire.

Snaring tactics
- look for a well-used trail
- find a natural narrowing in the trail
- select strong material
- ensure the loop closes smoothly
- secure the snare
- do not disturb the animal trail
- leave as little scent as possible
- widen the loop across the bottom
- ensure that non-wire snares lift the animal
- set lots of snares

Preparing your catch

Once you have caught an animal, you must immediately clean it and cook or preserve it. Preparing an animal for dinner is pretty simple: remove outside; remove inside; cook; and eat.

Waste nothing in survival. If you are lucky enough to catch an animal, do not discard the hide and the innards. The guts will make fine bait for birds or fish and the hide has many uses such as:
- water containers
- clothing

Preparing a rabbit for eating

Pinch and pull to open

Remove everything inside from these points

Survival Secrets

- lines for more snares
- materials for building snowshoes
- fishing line, bow string, et cetera
- thread to make or repair clothing

The fur-covered skin peels off easily, particularly when the animal is warm and freshly killed. Use your thumbs and forefingers to pinch open the thin soft belly. Remove the stuff that does not look like it came from the meat section of the grocery store. Everything comes out easily and is only firmly attached at the extreme opposite ends. Cook and eat the remaining part.

Boil your catch in water if possible. You can then drink the broth or make stew if you have harvested edible plants. If you do not have a container to boil the animal you should cook it in front of the fire rather than over the fire.

Cooking your meal

There are several reasons to cook in front of rather than above your fire. Conifer wood smoke (from pine, spruce and cedar) will impart a bitter resin taste to an otherwise tasty meal. Cooking in front of the fire also reduces the risk of burning your hand. If your first meal in a week drops into the fire, you will not think twice about reaching into the fire to retrieve it.

If you have never eaten rabbit or squirrel you are in for a pleasant surprise. I have lost count of the number of times I have heard people describe their first meal of rabbit or squirrel as delicious.

A word about hunting...

Many people in our society are opposed to hunting; some are opposed to eating meat. If you hold these beliefs, I respect your right to choose how and what food arrives on your dinner table. However, if you are ever in a group survival situation, I hope you consider the following argument.

You must remember that rescuers put their lives at extreme risk. Regardless of your views on killing animals for sport or food, you have a responsibility and an obligation to make every reasonable effort to survive – including, in some cases, hunting, and eating your catch.

I also ask you to consider the well being of your fellow survivors. An openly expressed opinion against killing and or eating something from the wild might affect someone else's ability to participate. You might deny someone psychological as well as physiological benefits. Even an obvious lack of enthusiasm can adversely affect group morale and, ultimately, the will-to-live.

You are entitled to your beliefs – and your companions are entitled to survive. They should feel free to make every effort to extend their lives one moment longer. You must put your obligations to your fellow survivors above your beliefs about hunting and eating meat.

Survival review

Do not consider foraging for food until you have completed the survival plan!

Review the foraging checklist in this chapter and weigh the benefits and dangers of leaving camp to forage.

Survival Travel

Survival travel can be summed up in one word of advice: Don't! Rescuers usually find the site of the accident first and then have to look for the departed survivors. By the time the searchers find the victims, they have usually perished. Had they stayed put and implemented the survival plan they would have been rescued. Even when survivors reach safety on their own, the rescuers have usually long since found the accident site.

If you do choose to leave the accident site, you always have a better chance of being found or rescued if you leave a travel plan. Hunter safety training teaches "plan your hunt and hunt your plan." All outdoors and wilderness travel activity should adopt this philosophy.

> **Survival secret**
>
> Leave a travel plan.

Why travel in survival?

There are only a few good reasons for travel in survival.
- Safety (flood, slide, fire, weather, exposure, predators)
- Visibility (to see and be seen)
- Resources (fuel, shelter, signaling, water, foraging)

Before you leave the original accident scene you should use the survival plan as a checklist to evaluate your travel needs.

The best survival travel checklist
- **first aid:** are you capable of travel?
- **fire:** can you keep warm travelling and make a fire?
- **shelter:** is there enough daylight to travel and then find shelter before dark?
- **signals:** can you see and be seen while travelling?
- **water:** can you carry or find sufficient water?
- **food:** do you have enough energy or food to travel?

The following considerations can be added to your travel checklist.
- **location:** do you know where you are?
- **destination:** do you know where you are going?
- **direction:** can you set and maintain a course?
- **clothing:** is your footwear and clothing adequate?
- **equipment:** do you have enough equipment? Do you need what you are leaving behind?

After you review the above checklist you will probably realise that the best chance for survival is to stay where you are.

Direction finding

If you must travel you will have to be able to set and maintain your direction of travel. There are many ways to set and maintain direction. The following is a list of some common aids:

- compass
- topographical map
- map and compass
- sun
- stars
- moon
- stick and shadow
- watch and sun
- rivers
- shore line
- ridges
- wind lanes
- GPS
- trails, railway tracks, power-lines

Survival review
- plan the trip
- leave a message with intentions, date and time, condition, and equipment
- pace yourself
- avoid night travel (except in a desert)
- do not challenge nature
- rest regularly and assess your condition and progress
- make camp before dark
- blaze or mark your trail so it can be seen coming and going

It would require an entire book to adequately address wilderness travel and navigation. This is one area where a little knowledge can be a very dangerous thing. Use the survival plan as your guide to assess travel requirements. By doing so you will likely come to the conclusion that travel is not your best choice.

Survival secret

It is almost always inadvisable to travel in a wilderness survival situation.

Survival Psychology

Research into all types of emergencies involving fire, earthquake, flood, and volcanic eruption, as well as sea, land, and air disaster, reveals a startling statistic. Approximately 80% of survivors are temporarily traumatised in the aftermath of an accident (this condition can last for only a few moments or up to several hours). Traumatised survivors often fail to comprehend or recognise a threat, and consequently fail to take immediate and decisive action.

Survival training sometimes fails to adequately address victim trauma. Many survival situations unnecessarily result in permanent injury or death because the victim has not been trained to function while traumatised. With proper training and psychological preparation you can take advantage of critical and fleeting survival opportunities. You can help yourself and others even if you are traumatised. In this chapter you will learn how to program yourself to function reliably in the event of any emergency, even in the probable event that you are traumatised.

The crash

Accident and other emergency victims frequently manifest behaviour that is ineffective or even life threatening. A prime example of this behaviour was observed during the aftermath of a military aircraft accident at my home base.

The aircraft broke apart during the crash. Two crew members were thrown clear of the aircraft and miraculously escaped injury. To the onlookers' surprise and dismay, the crew members walked over to the burning aircraft and climbed back on board. These otherwise uninjured aircrew members were seriously burned before the fire fighting team rescued them.

The actions of these two crew members seem incomprehensible, but there is a rational explanation for their behavior. After a normal landing the aircraft taxis into the parking ramp. Each crew member completes his or her respective shut down procedures. Finally the noisy engines wind down. Stillness and silence washes over the crew. The last thing a crew member does is un-strap and exit carrying his or her personal gear.

These survivors were traumatised by the crash. They were not psychologically prepared for the flight to end in a crash, and they could not comprehend that the flight was terminated. They climbed back on board the burning aircraft to retrieve their personal flight equipment. This action made perfect sense in their traumatised state. They were attempting to make the flight end normally.

Unfortunately the above-mentioned behaviour is the typical irrational response to catastrophe. During and after a mishap it is common and predictable for people to persistently continue with their original mission. They do this despite the inappropriateness and futility of these actions. Thus I cannot overstate the importance of learning how to function despite trauma. In a survival situation, lives may depend on it.

Dealing with loss of control

Survival emergencies force you to deal with "loss of control" over situations that you rely upon but take for granted. We normally maintain effortless control of light, heat, comfort, water, food, communication, and transportation. We exert minimum effort to control our environment. We utilise sophisticated clothing, housing, and transportation technology. Unfortunately, we have become overly reliant upon this complex but fragile technology. We also have come to assume that nothing bad will ever happen to us.

Loss of control in survival emergencies is frustrating, bewildering, and traumatising. Failure to overcome loss of control in survival is quite common. The result is devastating. The best way to regain control and ultimately to survive is to memorise a simple emergency plan that you are committed to initiate immediately and complete without deviation. By doing this you will have programmed yourself to function effectively despite trauma.

> **Survival secret**
>
> Most survival opportunities occur in the first few minutes after an accident! You must program yourself in advance to accept your survival circumstances immediately or you will likely miss those opportunities.

The unprepared accident survivor invariably loses precious time and opportunity by struggling through all of the post accident phases (shock, denial, anger, and acceptance). The advice in this book is designed to program you to accept an accident situation immediately. You will then be able to take advantage of fleeting but critical opportunities.

The will-to-live

The will-to-live is the most important factor in extending life in an outdoor survival situation. It enables you to conquer survival circumstances that involve harsh environmental conditions, injury, loss, and unrelenting discomfort. You can use the secret of the will-to-live phenomenon to battle any kind of physical or mental duress. For fifty years, survival training has taught that the single most important attribute in survival is the will-to-live. However, to use the will-to-live advantageously, you must understand it and know how to use it. This chapter will give you the tools and the knowledge to do just that.

Unravelling the "will-to-live" mystery

The will-to-live is a baffling enigma. In training, virtually everyone claims to possess the will-to-live. In actual survival situations however, people tend to succumb surprisingly quickly to unrelenting environmental exposure. In most survival crises, people actually die prematurely. They fail to extend life to its maximum limit. This tendency to expire quickly in harsh survival circumstances prompted me to research the will-to-live. The result was the discovery of what I believe is the most important survival secret, which is how the will-to-live extends survival and, more importantly, how anyone can invoke it.

The following case study helped me learn more about the will-to-live, and to arrive at a "will-to-live theory."

> A man in his mid fifties was driving through the desert. His vehicle broke down in the middle of nowhere. He was unfamiliar with the desert. He attempted to walk back to civilisation. It was the middle of the day and he was exposed to the blazing sun. He had no plan, no water, and no appreciation of the difficulty he was getting himself into. He was soon dehydrated to the point where he could not think clearly. He began to wander aimlessly but persistently.
>
> He was eventually rescued. He was found naked, crawling across the desert on his hands and knees. He had lost 25% of his body weight due to dehydration. Medical science contends that this degree of weight loss through dehydration should have killed him. He was so dehydrated that his many open cuts did not bleed.
>
> His ordeal and subsequent recovery prompted many questions. What was his secret? What had enabled him to live through an ordeal that medical science believed should have killed him? His story reveals the secret in both understanding and invoking the will-to-live.
>
> It turned out the man was quite wealthy and had recently married a much younger woman. Some may immediately think that burning love for his attractive young bride had provided incentive to return to her side. Actually, his marriage was failing miserably.
>
> However, there was another compelling motivation that drove his body beyond all medical comprehension of human limits. Early in his dilemma it occurred to him that if he perished, his children from a previous marriage would not receive their inheritance. His sizeable estate would go instead to his new bride. Throughout his ordeal, he constantly focused on one single, all consuming obsession. He just had to live long enough to change his will.

As this case study illustrates, the will-to-live means selecting, and remaining tenaciously focused upon one single reason why you must withstand your survival ordeal. You must maintain this focus no matter how much pain, suffering, and deprivation you experience. You should program yourself in advance to focus on one single idea. You must select one single compelling inspiration upon which you can concentrate. This motivation can be an unfinished achievement or a commitment you have made to yourself or to others. Applying this technique will significantly help you block out pain and suffering.

My will-to-live theory

I have developed a theory as to how and why single-minded concentration invokes the will-to-live and thus increases your survivability.

In a survival situation, continuous torment often persists without respite. Survivors often recall comrades who just gave up and then died shortly thereafter. Caregivers commonly make the following observation: "The light went out of their eyes, and moments later they were dead." There has been no medical explanation given as to why one survivor lives, while their companions succumb to exposure from the same elements.

It would appear that your body's automated systems begin to shut down when certain criteria are met. This includes giving up hope of rescue or suffering constant torment. I believe that your mind has the ability to over-ride those shutdown thresholds. You can reject Mother Nature's well-intentioned gift of premature death by invoking the will-to-live.

In order to cheat death you must concentrate and remain focused on one single reason for extending life. This single-minded focus enables the brain to over-ride normal shutdown thresholds. Your reason for extending life must be your special reason: it does not have to be important to anyone but you. The message your body receives is simple, "Do not shut down! Keep operating!"

Regularly assess your special reason to survive. Teaching you how to maximise your will-to-live is the most important survival advice offered in this book.

Survival secret

Invoke the will-to-live.

There are survival benefits, in addition to invoking the will-to-live, that you can gain by learning to control your autonomic systems. I learned to control heart rate and breathing while practising drown proofing. (Drown proofing is no longer taught because the required movements cause an accelerated loss of body heat.) I was able to focus on and slow my heart rate, which was audible under water. The slower my heart beat, the longer I was able to extend the interval between breaths. I was then able to remain submerged for much longer periods

This technique was invaluable in subsequent underwater escape training. I found myself capable of performing complicated and lengthy escape procedures that mystified instructors. Knowing how to maximise your survival capabilities in an actual underwater emergency boosts your confidence. There are many situations where consciously reducing heart and breathing rates would prove beneficial.

Single-minded focus and the resolve to persevere account for success in areas other than survival. You will conquer many of life's challenges, including survival, by applying the following principles:
- commitment
- concentration
- focus

Psychological problems and solutions

In any survival situation you will have to overcome some degree of psychological difficulty. You must learn to recognise, understand, and deal with common psychological survival problems.

Fear

Survival implies an immediate threat to your life. Hopefully you will be aware of your survival predicament. You will experience fear, which if uncontrolled, will lead to either panic or trauma. Either of these reactions will cause irrational behaviour and prevent effective problem solving. You must understand fear and learn how to control it.

There is an upside to fear in survival. Fear produces adrenaline, which can save your life.

How to conquer fear

First you must recognise your fear. Then you must confront it and put it in proper perspective.

Typical survival fears

There are a variety of fears commonly experienced in survival. These fears are in addition to the initial fear associated with the event that caused the survival situation. These can include:
- fear of facing your dead companion's loved ones
- concern for the welfare of your family or loved ones
- fear of causing worry and anguish in others
- fear of embarrassment
- fear of career or monetary consequences

Do not become distracted with concerns that are beyond your immediate control in a survival situation. It is natural to worry about the anguish your situation is causing others. It is natural to feel guilt if you have made a mistake. But remember, no one wants you to die because you have made a mistake. Rescuers are likely risking their lives on your behalf. No one should risk his or her life to haul out a corpse. You have a responsibility to survive. Concentrate only on your survival. If you initiate the survival plan immediately, you will be too busy to worry about things that are beyond your control.

In summary, survival often hinges upon one tiny inspiration that snatches victory from the jaws of defeat. If your mind is occupied with futile concerns, you might overlook an opportunity. Resolve to concern yourself only with survival and suppress concerns over which you have no control.

Phobia

A phobia is a fear that is unreasonably disproportionate to the actual threat. Phobias can be completely incapacitating. They can prevent you from dealing with more serious threats. You may not even be aware that you have a phobia until you are actually in a survival situation.

Stressful situations will exaggerate the effect of a phobia. Survival certainly qualifies as a stressful situation. By controlling your phobia you will be able to recognise a real threat and react appropriately. The following is a list of common phobias experienced in survival:

Common phobia
- being lost
- being alone
- predators (real) such as bears, wolves, cougars
- predators (imagined) such as vampires, ghosts
- dead bodies in group survival situations
- the dark
- wilderness or open spaces
- water and things in the water
- heights
- bats, snakes, spiders and other creepy crawlies
- noises such as owls, coyotes, and wolves
- things that go bump in the night
- your personal demons

Any phobia could threaten your survival. It must be confronted, rationalised, and placed in perspective relative to your survival situation.

Phobic reactions often degrade the student's survival training benefit. Deal with a phobia by acknowledging it publicly. Talk openly about your fears. Everyone has experienced phobias. You can expect helpful support and encouragement.

"The Hump"

I was contracted to teach survival to a group of tree planters who were preparing to spend the summer in the mountains of Alberta and British Columbia. One third of this group was experienced and the remaining two-thirds was novice. I was lecturing on outdoor safety and survival, including bear awareness. The previous year a bear had false charged members of the group on two occasions. Fortunately these were just threats or false charges. The veterans had exaggerated the bear encounters to impress the novices.

Introducing the subject of bear awareness prompted immediate nervous glances and whispering between novices. This was ample indication that bear concerns had probably reached phobic levels with some of them.

I could see that the experienced veterans of this group were visibly bored with the prospect of basic bear training. They had already survived an actual encounter. The novices would believe that my bear training was worthwhile only if the veterans expressed interest. I had to convince them that bear attacks are survivable.

The most effective way to validate a teaching point is to elicit testimony from within the group. I began by explaining that your actions in the event of a bear attack depend on the type of bear. Is it a black bear or grizzly bear? I asked a novice for a reliable recognition feature. He suggested colour. I paused and pretended to weigh the merits of his suggestion thoughtfully. The veterans knew that both blacks and grizzlies appear in a variety of colours. My hesitation was causing serious doubts regarding the value of my impending bear advice. I obviously had never seen a bear.

After the lengthy pause I asked one of the veterans if he could provide a more reliable method of bear identification. "The grizz has a hump," he quickly volunteered. He attempted to describe a hump by drawing a picture in the air with his hand. You could sense that he had not given up hope that I might actually know what a bear looked like. Perhaps a visual reminder would jog my memory.

I gave him a look of wonder and amazement. I slapped my hand to my forehead and exclaimed, "The hump! Of course! The hump!" You could see the relief on his face. At least I knew that the grizzly had a hump. I responded with, "That's a lot better than the method I was going to recommend. I was going to tell you to climb a tree. If the bear climbs the tree and eats you, it's a black bear. If the bear pushes the tree over and eats you, it's a grizzly." The veterans and novices both laughed. I now had everyone's attention and participation.

I pointed out that they had just laughed about bear attacks. I went on to explain that being able to laugh is the first step on the road to "wrestling" this bear phobia into submission. (Mentioning the word wrestling in the same sentence as bears caused some students eyes to approach the size of saucers!) I needed to identify those students harbouring deep-seated bear phobia.

Fear of the unknown

Some phobias truly defy logic. Fear of the unknown is common in survival. Survivors waste fleeting opportunities because they are paralysed by groundless fear that has no identity.

The key to avoiding fear of the unknown is knowledge and experience.

Participating in survival education and training will help you avert fear of the unknown. Learn how to recognise and cope with real threats.

Group psychology

Many survival situations involve groups. It is important to understand group survival dynamics. Survivors who manifest inappropriate behaviour may simply be traumatised or under stress. You can help everyone by providing tactful guidance.

The most effective survival leadership often comes from calm, confident, and quiet individuals who are not normally viewed as leaders in ordinary circumstances. In providing survival leadership you must speak with conviction and authority to ensure others will respond. Be firm and precise, and provide simple instructions that are easily understood and easily performed. Explain the benefits of following your instructions. Explain the consequences of not following instructions. Utilise teamwork whenever possible to ensure success and avoid weak links. Establish the buddy system and ensure that it is faithfully followed.

Dealing with difficult people

We have all had experiences where an irritating or unco-operative personality has created problems within a group. If the situation is not dealt with tactfully and promptly, it can result in open conflict or even retaliation. In a group survival situation, it is critical that undesirable behaviour be resolved promptly. It helps if you are prepared in advance to recognise and deal with these situations.

Use tact and diplomacy, and do not be overly critical. Start by telling the problem individual how things should be. "We are in a tough situation and we all must co-operate and work together if we hope to survive." Anti-social behavioural problems in survival that are not addressed will likely result in serious and escalating difficulties.

Group survival attributes

- responsibility and teamwork
- positive attitude: acknowledge and encourage every effort and achievement. Project optimism and hopefulness
- communication skills: listen and speak carefully, be prepared to take as well as give direction
- teamwork: your group is as strong as the strongest link with teamwork. It is as weak as the weakest link without teamwork. Overlap critical functions to ensure success
- leadership skills: reliability, dependability, honesty, tact
- delegation: give responsibility and authority to the most capable people
- will-to-live: maximise this ability and tell everyone how to invoke it
- helping others: you may need help eventually, pay your dues in advance, what goes around also comes around
- irritating habits: avoid, tolerate, or tactfully address them
- compassion: reassure, treat special needs, use tact
- buddy system: establish and maintain this system

Survival review

In an actual survival situation you must be prepared to lose control over many things that are normally taken for granted. You must realise that you will be afraid and possibly even phobic. By training to recognise and function despite these problems, you can effectively prepare for a survival situation.

Large Predators

chapter 13

There are many dangerous animals in the wild. The mountain lion or cougar is making a comeback and occasionally preys upon humans. Wolves will attack humans in only extreme and unusual situations. I have been surrounded by a large hunting pack of wolves. They were each between three and fifty feet from me. At no time did they act aggressively and therefore I did not feel threatened.

In this chapter I will deal only with bears. They are the largest and most dangerous predator in North America. In bear country you are more likely to be struck by lightning than attacked by a bear. If you are attacked, it is vital that you remember to do everything in your power to extend life one moment longer. You must also apply the will-to-live. It will also be very helpful to have programmed yourself with bear knowledge and a plan of action.

Bears

I advise caution in dealing with bears. Bears are very widespread in the wilderness. Always assume that you are in bear country.

In a wilderness accident that involves fatalities you must immediately separate the dead from the living. Rescuers tell horrific tales about confrontational bears at fatal crash sights. The scent of blood and dead bodies is known to over-ride a bear's inherent fear of man. Bears will often stake a claim to a body, and they tend to be fiercely protective of their food cache.

Bears are very intelligent animals. They learn quickly from experience. They adapt to encounters with humans. When you come upon a bear, always assume that it has had negative experiences with humans and act with extreme caution. Bears are unpredictable and dangerous. Bear encounters rarely result in an attack. Nonetheless, you should not take any chances around bears.

A wilderness bear, black or grizzly, tends to be shy and normally runs at the scent of humans. Your best protection against bear attack is

Survival Secrets

to constantly make noise as you travel. You do not want to surprise a bear. Arriving inside a bear's flight or fight range unannounced is extremely dangerous.

Black bear

A wilderness black bear must overcome its natural fear of humans in order to attack you. If you surprise a black bear, it will usually run. If it runs towards you, it may not be attacking you. It may have smelled or heard you, but not seen you. You may simply be blocking its escape route. Even a deliberate charge is often a bluff. Do not turn and run! Running away often stimulates the attack instinct in a predator. Running away can turn a harmless bluff charge into a fatal attack.

In the unhappy event of a black bear attack, your best chance to survive is to rekindle the bear's natural fear of humans. The following recommended actions are often successful, though not guaranteed:

Fighting off a black bear

- Try everything possible to discourage the attack. Noise usually frightens and confuses black bears when they attack. (They depend heavily upon their sense of hearing and smell. Their snout will already be corrupted with your smell.) If you make sufficient noise you will block their ability to hear approaching danger. Yell continuously at the top of your lungs. Solicit help from Antarctica. Put anger not fear in your voice.
- Fight as hard as you can. Use any weapon you can reach. Target the snout, eyes, or anything vulnerable. Never stop fighting back. Your objective is to make the bear nervous and confused. Often these tactics will cause the bear to break off the attack.

Grizzly bear

Grizzly bears are territorial and aggressive. You should constantly make noise to avoid surprising all bears and especially grizzly bears. They are dangerous when guarding a food cache, feeding on prey, or foraging. It is strongly recommended that you wear a noisemaker. Many camping and outfitter outlets sell inexpensive bear bells.

Remember to put a bear bell on your dog. When your dog finds a grizzly it will likely run as fast as it can to seek protection between your legs. It will then bravely start barking insults and challenges. Climb a tree when you hear a bear bell approaching at a hundred miles an hour. I guarantee that your dog won't stop to sniff you out.

Many wilderness park bears have lost their fear of humans. Their behaviour is impossible to predict. If you are confronted with a threatening grizzly, do not look directly at the bear. A human has the close-set eyes of a predator. Staring straight at the bear will be interpreted as a territorial challenge. Turn your head so that the bear can see only one eye. Look down and away from the bear, but keep one eye on it at all times. Hopefully that last bit of advice strikes you as unnecessary. Adopt a subservient posture; use body language to let the bear know that it is the supreme ruler of the universe.

Do not turn your back on the bear! Turning your back often triggers an attack response. Back away slowly until you are out of the bear's sight. Once out of sight you will probably feel like running. Be careful not to rush headlong into a second bear.

Fetal position with grizzly bear watching after attack

Arms and knees over gut, lie on side, breathe very slowly after Grizzly attack.

If a grizzly attacks you, do not expect to see it rise up on rear legs with threatening growls and gestures. You will more likely be subjected to a fast hard charge. Anticipate the initial attack, and fall down and away. This will help avoid having the wind knocked out of you. Lie on your side and remain completely still. Bring your knees up under your chin to protect your soft under belly and vital organs. Clasp the hand of your bottom arm over the back of your neck and position the top arm over your exposed side. You can also lie face down with both hands protecting the back of the neck and legs spread apart to prevent the bear from rolling you over.

The grizzly cannot open its jaws wide enough to crush your skull. That may sound like more than you need to know, but it is actually valuable information. The bear often rakes the skull with its teeth in a futile attempt to crush it. Fighting back is not generally a good option with a grizzly, unless you have bear spray or a potent and effective weapon. Struggling is liable to anger the grizzly and increase the ferocity of the attack. The bear may leave you alone shortly after the initial attack. Remain motionless on the ground. Bears are not malicious. They will not remain angry for very long. Remaining motionless will usually cause them to lose interest.

The initial grizzly attack is usually short in duration. This short period seems like an eternity (remember adrenaline puts events into slow motion). After the attack the grizzly will likely stay close by for a while and watch and listen for signs of life. You must remain lifeless as long as necessary to convince the bear that you are dead. The second attack is usually a lot worse than the first. Knowing this should provide the incentive to lie motionless. A grizzly may drag you to a new location and cover you with brush and even urinate on you to claim ownership. Play dead through all this.

Using pepper spray

You may purchase pepper spray for bear protection. Read the instructions before you go to the woods. Carry the can where you are able to reach it with either hand. Practice grabbing, aiming, and operating the bear spray without looking at the container. (When a bear attacks or confronts you, you will not avert your eyes to read directions or find the trigger!) Consider a two-second spray to create a cloud of pepper spray that might stop a charge. If this doesn't work, aim for the bear's eyes.

Both-hand bear spray

Survival review

The actions recommended herein are not foolproof. The ferocity and potential consequences of a bear attack must not be trivialised. It is important, however, to remember that people can and do survive bear attacks. You must reconcile any pain and injury connected with a bear attack relative to your future enjoyment of life. Survivors of bear attacks are always grateful to be alive!

If you are attacked by a bear, focus on a single reason for surviving. This will maximise your will-to-live. Adrenaline will block pain and help you to endure the attack. With proper awareness and preparation you will develop the confidence and determination to survive a bear attack.

Surviving Insects

chapter 14

Biting and stinging insects such as the black fly, mosquito and the tiny sand fly or no-see-um are more than just nuisances. They are serious threats to your survival. They are demoralising, distracting, and persistent. Your eyes may swell shut and the resulting discomfort from itching, pain, and swelling can actually drive you mad (this is not an uncommon survival occurrence).

You can learn to cope with insects. I offer some remedies here: test them on your next encounter with these tormentors.

The following story illustrates the benefit of learning to cope with flies.

While fly-fishing in Labrador, I was waist deep in a swiftly flowing stream, watching the surface intently. I was engrossed in a search for telltale rise forms that indicate the location of feeding trout.

I heard a faint voice over the noise of the rapids. I looked up and saw another fisherman approaching me. He spoke again but all I could manage to hear was the word repellant. I obligingly reached into my fishing vest and pulled out my insect repellant. I tossed it to him. He looked at the repellant, shook his head vigorously, and then threw it back to me. I shrugged my shoulders and returned to my fishing.

Later that evening this same fisherman approached me back at camp and asked if I was the person who had offered him the repellant earlier. I responded by suggesting that brand name loyalty to repellant manufacturers seemed out of place in the middle of Labrador. He explained that he had been offering me repellant, not asking for some.

Apparently the black flies had been swarming around me in such great numbers that he was unable to see my features clearly. I told him that I had been so totally absorbed in fishing that I was oblivious to the flies. He asked what my secret was for keeping the little pests from tormenting me. Judging by the respectful distance he maintained during our conversation I suspect he had already deduced that reducing bathing to a minimum was one of those secrets.

Bug secrets

Neutralising or at least minimising those things that attract flies to humans is the secret. They are attracted to you by:

- scent
- colour
- heat (infrared radiation)
- movement
- exhaled carbon dioxide

Flies are attracted by sweet cloying scents, such as after-shave, cologne, soap, or shampoo. The food you eat produces scent through your skin and your breath. When you eat bananas your skin and breath give off a cloying sweet odour that attracts insects.

Citrus fruits have a natural repellant in their peel called oil of citronella. Citronella was once widely used as an insect repellant and appears to be regaining popularity. Potent modern laboratory concoctions get mixed reviews concerning health safety.

Colour is a major factor in attracting insects. Lighter colours are the least attractive. Yellow is the best colour because it presents the least attractive wavelength to these insects. Some people swear that blue seems to attract flies. This may be another good reason to leave your blue jeans at home!

Swarms of flies and mosquitoes are very irritating. The more agitated you become, the more heat your body generates. Your body radiates excess heat by opening blood vessels in the neck, head, hands, and feet. This is one reason why insects appear to target the head and hands. Agitation also raises your respiration rate. Insects are attracted by the carbon dioxide you breathe out.

Movement attracts insects that might otherwise have passed you by. As you become progressively more agitated you tend to flail your arms around in a futile attempt to ward off the increasing swarms around your head. Flailing increases your production of carbon dioxide and heat, and your visibility.

The following story will illustrate the benefit in neutralising insect attractions. Many years ago, my wife and I were building a cottage in black fly and mosquito heaven (theirs, not ours). We took a break from our work and went for a walk along the edge of the nearby trout pond. As we walked through the long grass, clouds of mosquitoes and black flies swarmed around my wife's head. She soon became agitated and frustrated to the point of turning back.

We had been walking close beside one another. I pointed out that I did not have many flies around me. I gallantly offered my yellow nylon hooded shell jacket that I habitually wear in the outdoors. It is windproof, waterproof, and, most importantly, it is yellow. As soon as my wife put the yellow jacket on with the hood up, the swarms began to dissipate.

The colour had changed. The perfume and hair scent were blocked. As she relaxed, her heart and respiration rates lowered significantly, and she radiated less heat. Her exhaled carbon dioxide levels were reduced. Suddenly the world was transformed. Oppressive clouds of insects were replaced with sunshine, songbirds, butterflies, and wild flowers.

Avoiding insects

Black flies are active only during the day. They approach you by following your breath trail. If you face into the wind, you will find that most flies will swarm harmlessly in your breath trail, at the back of your covered head.

Mosquitoes are active day and night. Mosquitoes love dark, cloudy, moist days. They hide in the wet long grass and foliage. Mosquitoes are most active in low light conditions. They are particularly active in the evening. This would be an excellent time to stay close to a smoking fire or under cover.

Clothing

Dress properly to manage the black fly and mosquito problems. Black flies crawl into openings like loose sleeves, pant legs and collars. Seal all openings in your clothing. Cover your hands, head and neck (with mud, if necessary).

Mosquitoes can't penetrate thick, loose fitting clothing. The currently popular synthetic fleece materials provide excellent mosquito protection. They are also light and dry quickly, and they provide good insulation even when wet.

Insect repellants

There are many commercial insect repellants. Some of the most effective repellants will damage plastics! For health considerations, I choose to use them sparingly on my skin.

Most insect repellants lose their effectiveness quickly on your skin, especially when you sweat. Apply repellant to your shoulders and hat. These are the primary areas of heat production. A cloud of repellant will radiate around your head. This will help neutralise the attraction from both the heat and the carbon dioxide you produce.

Here's another trick that works very well. Put the repellant on your outer clothes and seal the clothes in a plastic bag. The repellant permeates the garments, and the treated outer clothing does not touch your skin. The repellant properties last much longer with this method. Repellant applied to your skin often dissipates within minutes.

Here is a trick for applying insect repellant. Put some repellant on the back of one hand. Then rub the backs of your hands together. Apply repellant to your neck, ears and face and any other exposed skin with the backs of your hands. This method will protect the plastics you touch, such as your fishing line, and you will avoid contaminating your food (the stuff tastes awful).

There are many non-commercial but nonetheless effective insect repellants such as citrus fruit skins (oil of citronella) and crushed cedar foliage. Smoke from fire, cigarettes, pipes, and cigars, also repels insects. But do not use survival as an excuse to smoke tobacco products! In survival, a dwindling tobacco supply is distracting and demoralising. The smoke from your survival fire, that you are supposed to keep burning at all times, is an equally effective repellant. Wind is a wonderful deterrent to insects. Select locations and activities that maximise the benefits of the wind.

Survival review

In survival, protection from and treatment for fly bites and stings is part of first aid. You must keep bites clean to prevent infection. Ammonia reduces itch and sting. I always carry a small perfume-sample vial of ammonia.

Survivors commonly delay or overlook insect protection. Unprotected insect exposure is a serious threat to your survival. Practising the suggestions offered here will enhance the enjoyment of all your summer outdoor activities. You will also be prepared for a survival situation.

After the Rescue

Post rescue collapse

Rescuers are trained to carefully scrutinise survivors who have been helping others through an ordeal. When rescue arrives it is common for survivors, who have been acting as caregivers, to relax. Ironically this can prove lethal. While they were completely focused on helping others, they had unwittingly invoked the will-to-live, which forced their bodies beyond normal expectations. When they relax, they tend to succumb to their injuries and deteriorate very quickly.

These survivors sometimes die before adequate medical treatment can stabilise them. Survivors who have been caretakers frequently require immediate first aid. They also need to be encouraged to persevere until first aid is administered.

Remember!

If you are a survivor, remain focused until your rescuers can adequately treat you.

If you are a rescuer, tell the victim to stay focused and to hang on until first aid is administered.

Post-traumatic stress disorder

Post Traumatic Stress Disorder (PTSD) commonly follows a survival experience. PTSD is a serious but treatable condition. Left untreated, however, PTSD can adversely and permanently affect your quality of life.

Look for the signs and symptoms in yourself or others in the aftermath of survival. Note that the symptoms may surface long after the event. Here are some of the indications that you or others may be suffering from PTSD:
- difficulty falling or staying asleep
- inability to concentrate or remain focused
- irritability

- easily startled
- reluctance to talk or think about the stressful event
- unwanted images, thoughts or perceptions related to the event invade your consciousness
- recurring dreams of the traumatic event
- flashbacks or hallucinations relating to the event

You should recommend or seek help if
- the symptoms persist for more than a month
- the symptoms affect relationships or work habits
- there is diminished interest in normally stimulating activities or events

PTSD is treatable but a potentially debilitating condition. If, after a month, you suspect it in yourself or others do not fail to take immediate action. Seek professional help from a counsellor, psychologist, or psychiatrist.

Test your Survival Knowledge

It's now time for you to test yourself. As you read these case histories, ask yourself what you would have done to
- avoid the threatening situation
- save yourself in the ensuing survival situation

Case #1: The novice boaters

The Smith family accepted a late season invitation to a friend's cottage. Because of the unseasonably warm fall afternoon they made a spontaneous decision to take the owner's powerboat out for a cruise. They had almost no experience with watercraft. They were soon several miles away from the cottage in an uninhabited portion of the large and unfamiliar lake.

Suddenly the motor stopped. It was an easily resolved problem. All they had to do was switch to the reserve fuel tank. But no one was familiar with the basic operator fault-finding procedures. Their only concern was returning in time for dinner. Nobody thought to paddle for the near shore, just a few metres away. The off-shore breeze soon pushed the boat far out on the lake.

Dark, threatening clouds appeared. The breeze quickly increased to a squall and the air temperature dropped. The skies opened up and torrents of icy rain began to pelt down. They were dressed for the earlier warm sunny weather and had not carried protective clothing. Wind and waves quickly combined to swamp the boat.

The capsised boat remained partially afloat. Initially they clung to the boat and to each other. One of the three children was eventually swept away in the heavy sea. Although wearing a personal flotation device, the child was unable to breathe in rough wind lashed surf (you can and should learn how to do this) and subsequently suffocated. The first casualty was claimed. The remaining survivors were blown across the lake with the mostly submerged boat, until they finally reached shore.

They were stranded across the lake in an uninhabited wilderness. Their debilitated condition numbed them to the loss of their child. They crawled ashore, battered, bruised, and exhausted, as well as cold, wet, and miserable. They huddled together as night fell and the temperature dropped. The weather had changed dramatically from what had been an unseasonably warm, autumn afternoon.

They made no attempt to start a fire or build a shelter. They were suffering from fatigue, hypothermia, and dehydration.

The storm prevented any effective search for over 24 hours. The following evening a co-ordinated air and water night-search was initiated. In the morning the family was found huddled together. None had survived.

Synopsis

Did you identify and consider these points?
- This was a spur-of-the moment trip and the family was not prepared for less than ideal conditions. They did not have an emergency plan. When the motor failed to start, no one in the group made an assessment of their predicament. They did not divide the duties or responsibilities. They just engaged in futile start-up attempts, wasting precious time. (In fact, the family was so engrossed in their efforts to re-start the motor that they failed to see that safety was within easy paddling distance. A well-traveled road was in full view on that side of the lake!)
- No one started a fire to combat the hypothermia – perhaps because they were traumatised, perhaps because they assumed that they needed matches. They could have easily started a fire using the boat's battery and fuel
- The family members' judgement was adversely affected by hypothermia, fatigue, and dehydration. They had an entire lake at their disposal but they did nothing to remedy their dehydration and thirst. They did not consider drinking from non-traditional sources

These were not stupid, drunken, irresponsible people. This was a spontaneous, unprepared family outing. The Smith family members were unfamiliar with the boat and the lake. The weather was deceptively balmy. These people were not prepared to recognise or deal with the emergencies they encountered. Minimal emergency preparedness training could have easily averted this tragedy!

Case #2: The professionals

Two professional outdoor instructors planned a one-day climb in the mountains. It was intended to be a morning climb and an easy afternoon hike down the opposite slope. Their day began several hours before daylight. They drove three hours to the base of their planned assent.

They arrived to find poor visibility caused by rain, snow, and fog. They had no alternative activity planned in the event of bad weather. They had invested a lot of time, effort, and expense to reach their objective. They decided to attempt the climb, hoping for a change in the weather.

Their wish for a change in weather brings to mind the old adage; "you should always be careful about what you wish for." The weather did indeed change. It got worse! Their ascent proceeded much more slowly than they had planned and at midday they finally recognised the futility of their endeavour. They attempted to back down the face but soon discovered that descent was far more treacherous than climbing. They were forced to climb. Darkness overtook them on the exposed mountain face. They huddled in misery through the night, exposed to the bitter cold and high wind. They had not come equipped for a night on the mountain. After a horrific night that less fit or determined individuals would not have survived, they doggedly continued their climb at daybreak. They finally reached the summit around mid-morning.

The relatively easy walk down the opposite side of the mountain should have taken just a few hours. They began their descent immediately, despite the continuing bad weather and associated poor visibility.

The poor visibility caused them to take a wrong turn. They didn't realise their mistake until the weather cleared. They had walked down the wrong side of the mountain. From this place, their only available route required them to climb back up and descend on the correct trail. Nightfall was approaching. They had descended into the tree line. They were surrounded with all the materials needed to make a warm comfortable camp and rest for the night. They chose instead, to immediately begin their climb back up in the dark.

They struggled throughout the night and by morning they had reached the summit once again. The weather was now clear and very cold. Without pausing, they began their final descent down the now plainly visible, but deeply snow-covered trail.

Just as they began their final descent, a search helicopter appeared overhead. Failing to account for the deep snow, they mistakenly believed they had an easy, two-hour, walk remaining. With so much effort and suffering behind them, they were now determined to finish what they had set out to accomplish. They waved off the helicopter.

Their progress through the deep snow was much slower than they anticipated. It was after nightfall when they finally reached the bottom. A sizeable group had gathered to welcome their triumphant return. A combination of embarrassment and false bravado likely caused them to delay seeking immediate medical assistance, which in turn caused them to loose several fingers and toes.

Synopsis

Where did these experienced outdoors instructors go wrong?

- These climbers did not have an alternative plan. Many of their early decisions were ill-advised and based on an overestimate of their ability to bend nature to their will. They decided to climb regardless of the threatening weather because of the time, cost, and effort, invested in the project. Alternative plans are necessary in any outdoor undertaking. The press-on-regardless attitude is historically responsible for many tragedies (not withstanding the odd Christopher Columbus). Such an attitude was very evident in this case. People sometimes risk safety for good or compelling reasons. This was not one of these occasions. This was not an adventure intended to make them rich or famous, but merely a one-day recreational climb. In the course of pursuing a routine outdoor adventure they committed the cardinal outdoor sin: they challenged nature!

> **Survival secret**
>
> Never challenge nature.

- Their next mistake was not being prepared for a night on the mountain face. Even with good weather, an injury could have delayed their progress. The following survival adage is equally valid whether planning outdoor activities or dealing with an actual survival emergency.

> **Survival secret**
>
> Hope for the best, but prepare for the worst.

- When they initially reached the top they did not assess the situation, attend to their injuries, build a snow shelter, or wait out the storm. They opted instead to immediately proceed in bad weather and poor visibility. At this point they were fatigue-impaired, dehydrated and in the initial stages of hypothermia. Normally hypothermia would produce telltale shivering, but not in this case. Their bodies had used up their reserves of stored glycogen and were consequently incapable of shivering. Signs of hypothermia, other than shivering, require specific knowledge and training to detect.

- The debilitating effects of fatigue, dehydration, and hypothermia diminished their capacity to think and solve problems. They tenaciously persisted in following their original plan. From the beginning they should have been regularly checking on each other, particularly for frostbite. They should have consulted with each other regarding the satisfactory progress of the current plan. They should have considered alternatives as each difficulty was encountered. They would have benefited greatly from following the rule of mutual and group outdoor activity. Remember:

> **Survival secret**
>
> Always use the buddy system.

- The climbers were not trained to assess their debilitated condition and take appropriate action. Alternatives, such as building a snow shelter and waiting out the storm were simply not part of their preparedness programming. Effective, analytical problem-solving abilities are not attributes commonly associated with fatigue, dehydration, and hypothermia. When they realised they had descended down the wrong side of the mountain, they failed to recognise the opportunity or the requirement to make a warm comfortable camp.
- Waving off the helicopter was a combination of false bravado and faulty reasoning. The debilitating effects of their ordeal had seriously impaired their ability to make sound decisions. They refused help because of pride and lack of personal and mutual assessment. They were reluctant to give up after so much effort and suffering when victory was apparently within their grasp. Failure to reconsider objectives was a serious problem throughout their ordeal.

> **Survival Secret**
>
> Regularly evaluate your progress and objectives.

- Finally, the two climbers failed to seek immediate medical attention. Remember: there is no shame associated with seeking help; it may save your life!

In summary, these two climbers failed to take advantage of numerous warnings and opportunities. To their credit, lesser individuals would not have survived the ordeal. They had plenty of outdoor skills, but they lacked adequate survival knowledge. These were outdoor educators! This case clearly illustrates the need to improve conventional outdoor safety and survival training. (I am certain that anyone who reads this book will learn how to avoid the mistakes outlined in this case history!)

Afterword

Survival students are usually exhilarated when they emerge from their wilderness training. They have proudly triumphed over nature's obstacles. Many of them experience adventures that extend their personal limits beyond anything they had believed themselves capable.

An aircrew graduate had just completed a two-week bush survival course. He was brimming with enthusiasm. He asked his instructor "What would you personally do if your aircraft was forced down in the bush?" I cringed at this question. There is only one survival plan regardless of your experience or qualifications.

The instructor paused a moment, thoughtfully stroking his two week growth of whiskers. "What would I do first, after a crash or forced landing?" He mused. "Well, first I would get clear of the aircraft. Then I would sit on a log or something handy and I would smoke a cigarette while I calmed down and collected my thoughts. Then I would plan what I was going to do."

There are several things deadly wrong with this advice:
- you must physically burn off your adrenaline and use it to your advantage
- you must work off your adrenaline within the first fifteen to thirty minutes after the mishap or risk hypoglycemia or low blood sugar. This condition would make you lethargic and prone to remaining inactive. This would have tragic consequences

In all fairness to that instructor, conventional survival training does not adequately stress the importance of memorising and strictly following the survival plan. But you know better! I am sure that by now that I am speaking to the converted when I say that you must memorise the plan, initiate it immediately, and complete it without deviation.

Remember this last survival secret:

> **Survival secret**
>
> The survival plan is not a menu. It is a recipe to be followed to the letter.

You have learned how to survive and how to avoid potential life-threatening situations. By internalising the emergency and preparedness techniques featured in this book, you will gain confidence and hopefully be motivated to broaden your horizons. There is no reason why you should not enjoy our less traveled wilderness areas and experience safe outdoor adventure, even when events don't go exactly as planned.

I hope that the foregoing material has been helpful and informative. I would be pleased to provide information regarding current available training, lectures, seminars, consultations, and courses.

Brian Emdin
11 Kings Court
St. Albert, Alberta
Canada
T8N 5M1
Phone # (780) 459 1039
E-mail: bemdin@survival-secrets.com